The Change¹²

Insights into Self-Empowerment

Jim Britt ~ Jim Lutes

With

Co-authors from Around the World

The Change[12]

Jim Britt ~ Jim Lutes

All Rights Reserved

Copyright 2016

The Change

10556 Combie Road, Suite 6205

Auburn, CA 95602

The use of any part of this publication, whether reproduced, stored in any retrieval system, or transmitted in any forms or by any means, electronic or otherwise, without the prior written consent of the publisher, is an infringement of copyright law.

Jim Lutes ~ Jim Britt

The Change[12]

ISBN: 978-1-5323-2532-8

Co-authors

Bill and Cynthia Delaney

Alison Lalieu

Andrea Wilson Woods

Bill Leydic

Charlene Renaud

David Ribott-Bracero

Dawn Lee

Deborah Crowe

Lisa Rimas

Dr. Shahid Sheikh

Evelyn J Waterhouse

José Aarão de Andrade

Laura Thompson

Lora Lucinda Andersen

Maggie M.C. Slider

Stefan Ciesielski

Armin Kittl

Kelly Brown

Phil Bush

Yves Deceuninck

The Change **is proud to support Good Women International.**

Every five minutes, one American child (many as young as ten years old) will be abducted and trafficked into the sex trade. 274 children a day, 100,000 each year and that estimate could be low. The total current number of human trafficking victims in the U.S. alone reaches into the hundreds of thousands and worldwide into the millions.

All profits from the sale of Amazon Kindle electronic books are being donated to Good Women International, whose focus is on the prevention of sexual exploitation of young women and children. They support self-empowerment and educational programs worldwide designed to educate our youth to avoid becoming a victim. A recent successful project was an anti-trafficking curricula for our high schools which is now complete and being utilized in many high schools around the world.

Enslavement is a reality. It is documented and it is real. The question is: What are we going to do about it?

To make a donation to Good Women International, a non-profit subsidiary of Village Care International, go to: www.SupportGoodWomen.com. All donations are tax deductible under Tax ID #: 88-0471768. We welcome and appreciate your donations, no matter how small.

http://GoodWomenInternational.org

Note: *Donations are never for salaries, as Good Women is a volunteer organization.*

DEDICATION

This book is dedicated to all those seeking change

Foreword

Berny Dohrmann, Chairman of CEO Space International

To The Readers of *The Change* Series:

Jim Britt has been a mentor to *Chicken Soup* authors, and to some of the foremost thought leaders on earth. Jim Britt's groundbreaking work in *Letting Go*, releasing past traumas and betrayals in life to return once again to forward-looking manifestation within your full powers, has been instructing at leading *Fortune* companies and to standing-room-only seminars all over the world. For three decades, Jim Britt has been the "trainer of the trainers," of which I am only one. Jim has been an instructor at CEO Space, the most prestigious, hard to get into faculty on the planet, where he developed millions of dollars of resources as he assisted others to develop tens of millions of dollars for their own dream making. Jim is the most "unchanged by success and wealth" man I have ever known. He is an unselfish archangel, like in his book *Rings of Truth*.

Today, Jim Britt and Jim Lutes, along with many inspiring co-authors from around the world, bring a pioneering work to the market to transform your own journey into master manifestation. Their principles are forged on coaching millions on every continent. As you read, you are exploring self-development as the world has yet to practice. In fact, Jim and Jim's publications lead to this one APEX MOMENT. Everything you have done to date in your own life, everyone you have met, every lesson you have learned, has led you to this one GREAT life opportunity… the moment of your own transformation into ever-rising full potentials.

As a five-time best-selling author myself, as a filmmaker, and with CEO Space, you can imagine how fussy I am to write a foreword to publications in the self-development space. CEO Space was just ranked by *Forbes Magazine* as the leading entrepreneur firm, which hosts five annual business growth conferences serving over 140 countries. It was also named by *Forbes* as THE MEETING in the world that YOU CANNOT AFFORD TO MISS. The world today demands more than a reputation defender to secure your forward brand; it requires that you take responsibility for your own brand and reputation in life. This book will inspire you to do just that.

CEO Space International has supported launches for many amazing works, including Chicken Soup for the Soul; Men Are From Mars, Women Are From Venus; Rich Dad, Poor Dad; The Secret; No Matter What; Three Feet From Gold; Conversations With The King; and now the movies Growing Up Graceland and Wish Man (for Make a Wish Foundation); Outwitting the Devil by Napoleon Hill and Sharon Lechter; Tony Robbins' great publications; of course Jim Britt's best-selling book Rings of Truth; and so many more. The totals have reached more than 2 billion eyeballs! You can't play around with that Mount Everest of credibility that I guard like a bank vault!

You can therefore appreciate why I encourage 100% of our followers of all the publications named to BUY JIM BRITT and JIM LUTES' book series *The Change* as a customer recognition for your own ten-best close relationships or clients. But don't just buy this book; rather, I endorse that you buy 10, and you giftwrap them to acknowledge your most important top ten relationships in life or clients in business. By doing so, you will retain more clients and encourage repeat buying. You may also receive more referrals and strengthen each relationship. The laws of giving will come back to you 10 to 1. When you give freely, you will always receive a rain into your life just as you rain into the lives of those you treasure. Jim Britt, Jim Lutes, and the insightful and inspiring co-authors have given you in *The Change* series a great opportunity... more important than pouring ice water over someone's head on YouTube as a challenge for charity! The gift that keeps on giving begins when you step up and BUY 10, knowing you have been instrumental in inspiring 10 friends to live a better life. Together, we are going to reach 1 BILLION SOULS as we help Jim Britt, Jim Lutes, and their co-authors to achieve their goal to transform human consciousness in our lifetime. Like Zig Ziglar, Jim Rohn, the great Roger Anthony, and so many friends who have passed, my friend Jim Britt is now a historical event in every training, every publication, and every online work at CEO Space. If you ever have the opportunity, STOP YOUR LIFE and see JIM BRITT & JIM LUTES LIVE and you will thank me personally, I know.

Their work is powerful. You'll let go of the baggage you've been carrying around for years and learn to embrace everything that creates the future you want and deserve. As you close the pages of any of *The Change* books, you will say over and over again "THANK YOU Jim Britt and Jim Lutes for creating this work." You will gain a new life of super focus as never before and you will commence to master manifest in your own individual life as never before. *The Change* books provide tools to transform results for corporations, institutions, and individuals, and once applied it will be impossible to miss your future success in life.

In my opinion, there are only the following areas to embrace for each of us:

Spiritual oneness and balance

Recreational balance and nature

Relationship where *Perfection Can Be Had!* (my book)

Career attainment of goals that you, yourself, reset along the way

Parenting either directly or by embracing a child you adopt to mentor at any and every age in life

These perspectives come into alignment within the framework of Jim Britt and Jim Lutes' imagination, along with decades of human-potential work. My advice is this work is a "BUY 10 TO SHARE WITH FRIENDS" pledge. In fact, a billion readers is a global path that Jim Britt and Jim Lutes are going to achieve NEXT for the world common good.

Let's help in this quest, as both men unselfishly donate their only asset, their precious LIFE TIME, to elevate one life at a time to their full potential and greatness.

My final request to all those who are reading my foreword is that you DO IT NOW. When you think of the good you will be doing, just ask yourself, "How long will I make them WAIT?"

I'm buying my 10 today!

Berny Dohrmann

Chairman, CEO Space International

P.S. I so approve this message for all my readers and followers worldwide. CEO Space has helped authors break the book of all records a half a dozen times, which means the only record to beat can be done with the publication you are buying 10 of now. Together, we are going to set a global record with one publication. Make the PLEDGE and give the gift of personal development. DO IT TODAY!

Table of Contents

Contents

Foreword vii
Jim Britt 1
   The Predator and the Prey 2
Jim Lutes 13
   Your Vault 14
Bill and Cynthia Delaney 23
   The Power of Higher Expectations: Hope is Not Enough 24
   IGNITE YOUR DESTINY 30
Alison Lalieu 37
   UBalancer Solutions 38
Andrea Wilson Woods 47
   Better Off Dead 48
Bill Leydic 57
   Reflecting on Your Reflection 58
Charlene Renaud 65
   The Piñata Theory 66
David Ribott-Bracero 75
   A Fight to Change 76
Dawn Lee 85
   Transforming Pain to Purpose—The Road Less Travelled to Peace, Love, & Happiness 86
Deborah Crowe 99
   Inspiration Rx: Live Life. Be Yourself 100
Lisa Rimas 107

Path to Enlightenment 108
Dr. Shahid Sheikh 117
    Case Study: Critical Areas Leaders Must Practice in the 21st Century to be Effective 118
Evelyn J. Waterhouse 131
    Learning to Love from the Inside 132
José Aarão de Andrade 143
    How are you showing up in life? 144
Laura Thompson, ACC, CEC, ELI-MP 153
    The Art of Mindful Communications 154
Lora Lucinda Andersen 163
    A Love Note to All Humanity 164
Maggie M.C. Slider 169
    Realizations 170
Stefan Ciesielski 177
    "Burn the ships!" 178
Armin M. Kittl 189
    Dream Your Life and Live Your Dream 190
Kelly Brown 203
    From Fear to The Power of Love 204
Phil Bush 209
    Selling Begins at the Intersection of Urgency and Importance 210
Yves Deceuninck 221
    A Whiter Shade of Change 223
AFTERWORD 234

Jim Britt

Jim Britt is an internationally recognized leader in the field of peak performance and personal empowerment training. He is author of 13 best-selling books, including *Cracking the Rich Code; Cracking the Life Code; Rings of Truth; The Power of Letting Go; Freedom; Unleashing Your Authentic Power; Do This. Get Rich-For Entrepreneurs; The Flaw in The Law of Attraction;* and *The Law of Realization,* to name a few.

Jim has presented seminars throughout the world sharing his success principles and life-enhancing realizations with thousands of audiences, totaling over 1,000,000 people from all walks of life.

Jim has served as a success counselor to over 300 corporations worldwide. He was recently named as one of the world's top 20 success coaches and presented with the best of the best award out of the top 100 contributors of all time to the direct selling industry. He also mentored/coached Anthony Robbins for his first five years in business.

Jim is more than aware of the challenges we all face in making adaptive changes for a sustainable future.

The Predator and the Prey

By Jim Britt

Maybe you have dreams and goals, but somehow things are simply not moving in the direction you had planned? Or worse, maybe you've stopped believing that the life you've always wanted is even attainable?

Let me ask you. Do you see similarities between you and your parents? The reality is that DNA passes down through generations… you, your parents, grandparents, great-grandparents, and so on. You could actually track it right back to when your ancestors lived in a cave. And in order to survive, prehistoric man needed to be able to see an event and interpret it as danger or safe…immediately! They had two dominant thoughts, "kill something to eat" and "keep from being killed and eaten." And to some degree, we still have this mechanism of recognition in place today. We just don't view it the same way.

Something happens… and your brain stretches and searches all through your past networks… or dendrites, which are the memory channels woven throughout your DNA looking to match some sort of pattern so you can make an instant decision… is this safe or dangerous? The meaning you give something is based upon a constant comparison of your past experiences and DNA programming projected into the future with the anticipation or possibility of it happening again. Something happens and you immediately tell yourself a story about what it means. Remember, it's a made-up story in your mind. It's not real… yet.

So when you step into the future, you don't really step into an empty future, but rather into a future that is filled with interpretations about what happened in the past, and what could happen in the future if you proceed.

For example, a salesperson prepares her presentation. She is excited for that important appointment to make a sale, but instead of a sale she gets a very rude "no." Now the next presentation, she won't step into a blank future, but rather, first, she steps into a previous negative past experience. Put enough of these "no's" together and now the salesperson does everything in her power to avoid prospecting so she doesn't have to experience another 'no.' Again, the rejection had no meaning until she gave it one. She got a "no" and she made it mean something about her, when in reality it wasn't about her at all.

Imagine three circles. A circle on the left. In that circle something happens to you... broken marriage, lose money in a business venture. You decide what goes in there.

Now there's the circle on the right. This is where you gave what happened to you meaning. Examples...bad experience with last business. Business didn't work last time and may not work now. Marriage ended in divorce. I don't want that again. You gave whatever happened to you a meaning.

Now, the circle on bottom. You live your life as if your story is true. We live in a black and white world.

However, most live their life in the gray as if their story is true, when in reality, it's a made-up story created from past experiences. This is an example of inauthentic living. You are living as if your story is true and reacting accordingly. Everyone has a story, but the reality is that your story is in large part an illusion... it's a made-up belief. All beliefs are false until you decide they are true, but that doesn't make them true. But if you decide it is true, then it will be true for you.

Core beliefs work like sunglasses. Sunglasses change incoming light before it hits our eyes. The world does not change to a shaded image just because you put on sunglasses. Only your perception changes looking through the glasses. Wear sunglasses long enough and you will eventually forget you have them on.

That's how beliefs work as well. Believe something long enough and eventually you experience it as true. It then becomes a core belief. Core beliefs change how you see the world before you are even aware of seeing anything. And core beliefs also determine how the world sees you. That's right. The world sees you the way you see you.

On the other hand, this mechanism is critical for your survival because it separates things that might get you killed and eaten from everything else. In a sense, your core beliefs protect you. But not always, because you automatically filter everything that happens to you according to core beliefs, which may or may not be true. In other words, your core beliefs may not be taking you in the direction you want to go.

Prey animals cannot afford to not follow their core beliefs. Humans are no exception. The top priority our brains have is to keep us from getting killed and eaten...maybe not literally in today's world. But, you may fear getting killed and eaten by an audience when you step on a stage, or by a prospect when making a presentation.

These things represent predators waiting to invade your refuge and attack you if you leave yourself open, or you start to take a risk. Our brains are wired to fear monsters, noises, and dangerous situations, because that is what our ancestors had to do to survive.

Humans of all ages establish and stick to routines no matter what, so they can survive. We take comfort in our routines. This makes perfect sense.

For example, if a predator attacks at dusk, then its prey should be out and about during the day and asleep and out of reach at night. If a predator attacks at noon, then the prey would most likely be nocturnal. Sticking to this routine helps the prey stay alive. Our prey habits are all about avoiding predators, discomfort, or dangerous situations.

Humans are prey animals whose top priority is not getting killed and eaten, avoiding pain, or not getting hurt. We therefore form habits to help us survive and then stick to those habits no matter how inconvenient, uncomfortable, unrealistic, or awful they are. We learned over countless generations that straying from our routine puts us at risk. Our brain does everything in its power to keep that from happening. This is why people refuse to change until the pain of *not* changing is worse than the pain of changing.

We desire to change, but when faced with the pain of change we weigh out both sides—the pain of staying where we are and the pain associated with changing. Whatever causes us less pain is what wins out. But the question is, do you win, or do you continue living a life of more of the same?

Core beliefs form our entire reality from birth to death unless we take action to change them. The good news is that you can change your beliefs. We do it all the time. Remember, a belief is a made-up story. Want to change it, make up something new!

It's like earning a six-figure income for example. Once you hit it, it becomes a core belief, so you settle for nothing less. The catch is that changing your beliefs will force you to confront programming that your brain interprets as being essential for your very survival. This is why crash diets, New Year's resolutions, joining a gym, opening a savings account, cutting up the credit cards, and other drastic changes rarely last more than a few days to a few weeks. At some point, the desire for change surrenders to the brain's built-in attempts to keep you from getting killed and eaten.

How do you change a core belief? Make up something new, let go of all that doesn't support it, and stick to it until it becomes a core belief.

Remember, every life level requires a different you. Think about that...EVERY LIFE LEVEL REQUIRES A DIFFERENT YOU.

Just look at your own life. What are some examples of drastic changes you have attempted in your own life?

Change requires that you change your perceptions.

Imagine a gopher that hides from hungry birds during the day. Most gophers will not leave their burrows during the day unless some emergency happens. For example, flooding the burrow gives the gopher the choice of *certain* death by drowning or *possible* death by escaping. In this example, the risk of following the normal routine becomes greater than the risk of doing something different.

Humans work the same way, except that our fears are based on past experiences combined with future anticipations. These fears are not real. They are imagined. They are a made-up story based on past experiences and programming that are designed to keep us safe. Just like the gopher, we weigh out the pain of staying where we are, not taking a risk, staying where we are comfortable, versus doing something in a different way.

Our routines form what's known as our comfort zone. We refer to doing things we don't normally do as "leaving the comfort zone." How did you feel the last time you left your comfort zone? Maybe someone asked you to deliver a short speech to a group of your peers. You may have felt scared, nervous, insecure, and ready to bolt at a moment's notice. This is a perfect example of our prey instincts telling us to get back in our comfort zone as quickly as possible.

I remember my first experience speaking. I literally thought I would be killed and eaten! I was to speak for 20 minutes to a group of about 20 people. I prepared for a month. I must have written 20 pages of notes. I couldn't stop thinking about it. What might happen if I didn't do it right, or forgot what I was supposed to say, or I might say it wrong, make a mistake…the list was endless.

I was staying in a hotel the night before I was to speak. I couldn't sleep, for fear of being killed and eaten! I tried to think of ways I could get out of speaking. Nothing seemed to make any sense. Then I came up with the answer. I will have an accident on the way to the speaking engagement. Not a huge one. Just something small, but big enough that I could show my bent fender so it looked legit. I figured the accident would be less painful than speaking.

Just as I went for the door to leave for my accident, someone knocked. I thought it was probably housekeeping, so I opened the door. It wasn't housekeeping. It was my associate that had booked the speaking engagement for me. He said, "I came to pick you up." My first thought was "you are going to be in an accident."

I said, "I'll drive."

He said, "No I'll drive."

I said, "No I want to drive."

He said, "I'm parked in front of the door. I'm driving."

I thought, "Do I grab the wheel of his car and have an accident?" I decided not to do that, but to follow through with the speech.

We arrived. I felt like I wanted to throw up. I was terrified. I took a few deep breaths and started my talk. I spoke for 20 minutes and I have no idea what I said. When I finished, I immediately went outside and stood beside the car and did a lot of deep breathing to regain my composure.

"Never again" was what I was thinking. After a few moments, I thought, "I have one of two choices. Never do it again, or do it often until I got better at it." After a lot of mental back and forth, I chose the latter.

I was in charge of about 300 salespeople that did presentations for small to medium sized groups to sell seminar tickets for a Jim Rohn seminar. I put the word out that I was available to do up to three presentations a day to groups of fifty or more…which I did for the next five years. And after about 15 presentations a week, almost 3500 total, I finally lost my fear of being killed and eaten by an audience. I created a new belief, a program that was stronger that the old one.

The stronger the urge to get back to your comfort zone increases, the farther you stray. This happens because our brains are wired to learn and follow habits designed to keep us safe and alive. We do this by learning how our predators behave and then creating patterns to avoid them, even if our predators only exist in our imagination. Like the "no" that the salesperson gets over and over, until now they are afraid to even prospect. The "no" becomes the predator.

Like the person that has been hurt multiple times in a relationship. And now the thought of getting involved in another relationship becomes very scary.

The comfort zone is nothing more or less than behavioral boundaries set by your core beliefs that were either formed when you were too young to understand what was happening, or over a long period of time through repeated experiences.

Core beliefs form your entire reality from birth to death unless you take action to change them. The good news is that you can change your beliefs. We do it all the time. Just think of something you used to believe that you no longer believe. Do you still believe what you believed in high school? Once you got out into the real world, you most likely looked back and laughed at some of the stupid things you did and what you believed to be true and realized it wasn't true at all.

It's like earning a six-figure income for example. Once you hit it, if that's the case, now you believe you can, so you settle for nothing less. That's called creating a new belief. The catch is that changing your beliefs will force you to confront programming that your brain interprets as being essential for your very survival.

Again, this is why crash diets, New Year's resolutions, joining a gym, opening a savings account, cutting up the credit cards, and other drastic changes rarely last more than a few days to a few weeks. At some point, the desire for change surrenders to the brain's built-in attempts to keep you from getting killed and eaten, unless you decide and commit to experiencing the pain of change and you stick with it until you change.

Just look at your own life. What are some examples of drastic changes you have attempted in your own life? How have they worked out for you?

How can you change when you run up against instincts designed to keep you safe and alive? A prey animal needs to react to predators without question. And if you want change, you have to become self-observant to determine what you should act upon and what is old programming that no longer serves your greater good.

Indecision causes hesitation. And if you hesitate, you could get killed and eaten! Hesitation gives predators an extra split second to move in for the kill.

It's starts with a decision to change whatever it is you want to change. So when one of those old programs arise, stop! Stop like you approach a red light at a busy intersection with a sign that reads "right turn on red after stop." Stop and ask yourself. "If I proceed, will this take me in the direction I want to go? Is this fear real or in my imagination, based on old programming?"

Take a good look at any animal whose parents raise the young. The young stick around to learn the survival skills they need to stay alive. Prey animals learn when they can come out, where to go, how to avoid predators, and when to retreat back home. Their survival depends on absorbing this information and mastering the skills without question. We were taught similar things. "That's hot, don't touch that, you'll go blind." "Careful, you'll fall."

Of course certain things we have learned have become essential to our survival. But unlike prey animals, we humans are programming our young from birth till they leave home, good or bad, right or wrong.

We are programmed about money based on how rich or poor our parents were and how they handled money. We were programmed about relationships, good or bad, based upon our parents' relationship. We were programmed regarding our eating habits, how we think, attitudes, and so on…good or bad.

Again all beliefs are false, until we decide they are true. The dictionary defines belief as, "to hold an opinion." We are programmed and convinced that our beliefs are true, whether they are true or not. In other words, we see and experience our beliefs as true. Two plus two equals four because we believe it does. If you believe that two plus two equals five, then no amount of argument will convince you otherwise, unless you choose to change that belief.

Beliefs equal truth because they are the mental sunglasses that filer your senses before you perceive the sensation. Your reticular activating system selects which sensory input is important based on your beliefs. Change a belief, and your view of the world changes, as well as the view others have of you.

Your beliefs color every bit of the input you receive. Only when you believe something do you become aware of the sensation of the input.

If our personal reality is based on core beliefs, then the universe that each of us experiences is not the cause but rather the effect of whatever is left over after our core beliefs do their work.

The statement, "I'll believe it when I see it" is backward. We actually see things *because* we believe them.

This has some amazing implications when you start to look at life in this way. Think about it. We see things *because* we believe it. Back to what I said earlier. When you change a belief, your view of the world changes.

So what is the answer to changing? The answer, or rather the challenge, is to take the negative past out of the present. The real goal should be to have your present empty of the negative past, and not to give your past meaning unless <u>you</u> say so.

Self-observation is the key.

Is what I'm giving energy right now taking me where I want to go? Is this fear or conflict supportive or non-supportive? Bottom line— is it true, or is it something you have been programmed to believe is true?

To change a belief, you have to challenge it.

Is it true?

What experience do you have that makes it true?

How do you know it to be true?

Who taught you to believe this?

What if they didn't know?

What if it's not true?

Who would you be without this belief?

What action should I take next?

When you achieve this level of control, you will experience what is known as true emotional freedom.

You'll have the freedom to choose fascination over frustration, success over failure, calm over upset.

When you take responsibility and observe reality… in other words what's really happening, you can then choose to create whatever reality you want.

Start today, by identifying a story you have been telling yourself that has been holding you back in life.

I can't get ahead financially. That's a story, not reality. It is not true unless you say it is.

I can't seem to keep a relationship together…

It's hard to lose weight…

Pick a story, just one to start. Look for the truth, then take action based upon that truth. The question is, does your interpretation of this story serve you or hold you back? Notice what you say to yourself about what has happened, and then exercise the freedom to choose a different interpretation.

I don't want you to believe me. I want you to try it and experience the result for yourself. You'll experience a positive result the very first time you try it.

Hey, and watch out for those predators!

***

To contact Jim:

www.JimBritt.com

www.PowerOfLettingGo.com

www.CrackingTheRichCode.com

www.FaceBook.com/JimBrittOnline

Jim Lutes

Having taught his branded form of human performance since the early 1990s, Mr. Lutes has accelerated top-level entrepreneurs throughout his career by conducting trainings on personal growth and subconscious programming into worldwide markets.

During this time, Jim took his skills regarding the human mind, and combining it with trainings on influence, persuasion, and communication strategies, he launched Lutes International in the early 1990s. Based in San Diego, California, Jim has taught seminars for corporations, sales forces, individuals, and athletes. Having appeared on television, radio, and worldwide stages, Jim's style, knowledge, and effectiveness provide profound results.

"Jim Lutes possesses a unique ability to create performance change in an individual in a fraction of the time it takes his competitors." The core of human decisions is based on the programs we acquire, reinforce, and grow. Combining Jim's various trainings, individuals can reach new levels of achievement and fulfillment in all areas of life. The results are at times nothing short of astonishing.

Your Vault

By Jim Lutes

Your vault—that is, the subconscious mind—stores a wealth of information for you. All of your experiences, emotions, memories, things you have learned, things you have heard, things your parents told you, messages from the media, messages from society. It's like an endless movie reel of data and information. All of this is in your subconscious mind and is therefore capable of influencing you in subtle and large ways. What is influencing you internally, or what I call your "internal influence," is impacting you more profoundly than you realize. The internal affects the external, so you can directly see the impact of your internal influence through what is happening to you and around you. Your internal influence is something to learn to be aware of—changing this will surely change what comes to you in your external environment.

There is one person you are with your whole life and that is you. Wherever you go, there you are. You are always with yourself. Keeping this in mind, are you aware of how you think? Have you noticed how you talk to yourself? Have you noticed how you react when you make a mistake, or things don't go your way? The tendency is to blame ourselves, or get mad at ourselves, when we make mistakes. Of course, some people project the blame onto others, but don't be fooled—they are still blaming themselves. Many of these tendencies and cues have been gathered throughout the course of your life via your subconscious mind. Your inner 'movie reel' collected all of your life experiences and all of those messages and then designed a script that runs in your head. This script is married to that sense of safety and predictability that we talked about earlier. It repeats information that it thinks will help you maintain a known identity, so that you do not have to experience stepping out into an unknown identity. Have you ever wanted to step outside of yourself completely? Have you accepted that this is not possible? Of course it's not possible to disengage from yourself completely. However, what *is* possible is that you can change this internal script! You can re-program the thoughts and ideas you loop internally to deeply affect life in every way imaginable! You, along with everyone else on the planet, have access to this magical portal. Yes, that's right, it's your subconscious.

This is neither about loving yourself, nor is it about ceasing to hate yourself. This is, however, about recognizing how you affect your behavior through your thoughts and beliefs and getting present to the fact that you do. The more you gain awareness of your conscious thoughts, the more you can rearrange those thoughts to be positive and affirming, signaling the same to your subconscious. This puts you on the path to becoming an ally to yourself instead of continuing to be your own adversary. If you are struggling and life is always miserable for you, take a look at your thoughts and you will find the root of your struggle. If you think you can't change your thoughts, think again.

The choice between remaining a victim of limiting thoughts and beliefs or freeing yourself from these limiting thoughts and beliefs actually exists, and it's yours to be made. You are responsible for your internal environment, and therefore your external environment. Your internal environment greatly affects your life circumstances. In fact, your willingness and ability to relate, connect to, and design your interior life, by getting to know your own mind, is critical to changing your life circumstances. The trick is to learn how to get your subconscious on board, how to build and maintain that sturdy bridge between your conscious and subconscious minds with you as the director shifting in the direction of your dream life.

Despite all of the Universal Power accessible to us through the subconscious mind, it remains that the subconscious mind still contributes to holding us back. For, in that storehouse of all our experiences are also found all the patterns and beliefs that were given to us without our choosing them. I'm talking about all of the experiences you've had over the course of your lifetime. The subconscious mind, just like a sponge, has absorbed all of them. Whether from traumatic experiences during childhood or the programming from authority figures in your life, the majority of beliefs and patterns running from your subconscious were most definitely not chosen by you. What you can choose, however, is what thoughts are entering your conscious mind. You can become the discerning bouncer of the nightclub of your mind. The subconscious mind wants to make manifest that which the conscious mind is thinking, so the faster you get this concept and start working hard to armor your conscious mind with positive thoughts, the more you will be able to attract and create that which you desire.

It is important to distinguish who you really are in all of this. Are you your subconscious mind? Are you your conscious mind? Are you your identity (which was created out of your past and survival programming)? Are you your ego?

The ego is created from the first memories and events of your conscious mind. It is thus created from the outset, and, also from the outset, the ego created a barrier between you and the innate wisdom stored within the subconscious mind. Your ego rooted and solidified as your life wore on, and your patterns manifested as expected. You developed a set of characteristics and qualities that corresponded with your ego. This is mostly because you probably knew nothing else as you grew up, other than to perpetuate the patterns absorbed by the subconscious mind throughout your childhood. These patterns and programs are filled with defense strategies that are generated automatically whenever there is a threat to our identity. The ego is attached to the identity, commonly known as ego-identity, which also makes the ego not the full picture of who you really are. This is because you are not your identity! And you are not your ego. And you are not your ego-identity.

Contrary to popular belief, the voice in your head is also not you. The voice in your head is only a part of you. All the voice in your head knows it sees through the filter of the programming in your subconscious mind. We tend to trust the voice in our heads immensely, but it is not the seat of true wisdom for any of us. The voice in our head, what I will call ego, operates on the plane of logic and rational thinking, but is unable to access the more creative and wise aspects of the subconscious mind. The ego is a mechanism devised to help you survive through life on the physical plane. Much of our ego is constructed around a set of beliefs and ideas that are a direct result of our conditioning and our experiences. These, as we know, are formed largely as a result of external information and cues from those around us. The ego helps you interact with people and your experiences, like a mental point of reference or template. The ego also keeps the myth of separation alive for all of us. It tries to convince us that we are not all part of the universal ocean of oneness. The ego likes words like 'me' and 'mine' and it filters your experience through the smallest universe possible, the universe of 'me'.

Without being able to separate ourselves from our egos, we will never truly be able to see that we are entirely one with the universe. The ego is tenacious! It is as though it has a vested interest in convincing us that we do not have access to that infinite Universal Power that each of us does. How do we separate our sense of selves from our ego? Yes, you guessed it—by cultivating self-awareness. As we identify and recognize those underlying messages that come from our conditioning, we can begin to see that they are not actually who we are. You can relate to the ego as a necessary "cloak" of identity that enables you to be in relationship with yourself and with others, but never mistake it for your true *essence*. Through developing self-awareness, becoming aware of your own thoughts, patterns, and habits, and then actively choosing to replace the old programming with newer supportive information, you can shift your relationship to your own ego. You remove the ego from the driver's seat! By doing this, we put our connection to Universal Power, our sense of ourselves as omnipotent, in front of the wheel. When we take the ego out of the driver's seat, we give ourselves the opportunity to build a stronger connection to our subconscious mind, that limitless vault of Universal Power.

Tangled up in our manufactured identities and the surviving ego is our self-esteem. We often seek help improving our self-esteem and self-image by reading books, or turning to programs developed and run by experts in personal development. What I have learned in my years of personal development work is that the only way to improve self-esteem and self-image in a deeper, more integrated way is by turning to world-class subconscious reprogramming techniques. We must connect to and re-wire our subconscious mind in order to create a new foundation for our lives. This is the seat of our access to change and our ability to shift the course of our lives. There is no self-help book in the world that you can just read that will suddenly give you high self-esteem. You have to practice and implement the techniques daily, regardless of the book, program, or teacher, in order to affect change. When you choose to work with your subconscious mind, however, you will get more effective results much faster. It's like choosing to fuel your car with the highest octane, purest source of gas versus going for the usual, run-of-the-mill unleaded variety. Sustainable, potent, and rapid change comes from choosing and committing to work directly with your subconscious. When you do this, your life course changes rapidly and with more ease. Simple, effective, world-class tools and techniques will be revealed to you so that you can begin to chart the course of your life according to your wishes and dreams!

Having a healthy self-esteem begins in your childhood. Self-esteem is about how we value ourselves. It determines how we perceive our value to the world and how valuable we think we are to others. Self-esteem affects so many parts of our lives, including our trust in others, our relationships, our work—virtually every part of our lives is impacted by how we bring ourselves to each interaction. Self-esteem is a core part of the mechanism that directly influences our sense of belonging, and how we relate to others. Self-esteem is directly connected to our sense of self-respect and self-satisfaction, and is expressed as having a sense of confidence. There is a spectrum of self-esteem states, and we can shift between them, from one to another. Positive self-esteem gives us the strength and flexibility to be the ones in charge of our lives. Positive self-esteem supports our ability to grow and our capacity for resilience, and enables us to move beyond fear of rejection and view mistakes as opportunities for growth.

On the other side of the spectrum is poor or low self-esteem. Authority figures in our lives—parents, teachers, and bosses—had a huge impact on how our self-esteem developed. If you were raised with parents who neglected you, boom! There goes your self-esteem. If you were raised with parents who doted on you, boom!

There goes your self-esteem in the opposite direction. If you had a parent of the opposite sex treat you differently in any way, this can affect your self-esteem. Particularly if you are a woman and your father did not help you cultivate your self-image, your self-esteem may not have risen to the level it should have. If you went to school and your teachers made a comment that you were not smart, boom! There goes your self-esteem.

Sometimes, the example of a balloon is used to illustrate our self-esteem. When we receive excessive praise or admiration for work that we have done, our self-esteem can over-inflate, like a balloon with too much air or helium inside. People with excessive self-esteem can become boastful or smug, sometimes trying to convince others of their own superiority. When we take in excessive criticism or hurtful comments about our work or behavior, we can develop poor self-esteem, like a deflated balloon. Having poor self-esteem can make us feel as though we don't have value in the world and that the work we do doesn't matter. Sometimes this can lead to self-destructive or self-defeating behaviors. No matter what the interaction, how big or small, your emotional reaction at the time of the experience would have been felt by the subconscious mind and the memory of this is still held in your vault. These memories contributed to you having a healthy balanced self-esteem, an excessively high self-esteem, or a poor or low self-esteem.

Each of these conditions has an immense impact on how we perceive ourselves in the world, influencing our sense of value or sense of worthlessness. What can you do about this? First, as I've mentioned previously, you must determine where your self-esteem is on the self-esteem spectrum. Then, decide to change your self-esteem back to a higher, but balanced place. How? You reprogram your subconscious mind, giving you access to the memory that initially helped to create your self-esteem, and then by separating out the emotion that was initially attached to the experience. You want to be able to have the memory, but to have it in a more neutral way, without so much emotion 'clouding' your memory of the experience. When you remove the emotion from the experience, you give yourself the opportunity for a new perspective of who you are, thus enabling you to directly increase your self-esteem.

Why is good self-esteem important, anyway? I know, it's a rhetorical question. Self-esteem is directly related to our internal set of expectations about ourselves. Good self-esteem is what will get you to take action in your life—and you only get results by taking action. I mean it when I say that there is absolutely no use for low self-esteem. Low self-esteem serves to keep you stuck in limiting patterns and perpetuates the victim mentality. Low self-esteem keeps you stuck in the mailroom when you belong in the corner office with big windows. Low self-esteem keeps you single when you know you have a lot of love to give and deserve a healthy relationship. It serves no one—and you serve no one when you are indulging in it. And yes, it is actually indulgent to wallow in a perpetual sense of low self-esteem!

That's right—I said it is indulgent to be stuck in low self-esteem. This is because ultimately, like anything, low self-esteem is a choice. If you suffer from low self-esteem, although you certainly did not choose to be imprinted with it or grow up with the experiences you had that created it, you are in your present life also not choosing to overcome it. This is how it limits you. If you really understand that you can choose to have high self-esteem, that having low self-esteem is not a curse or something you cannot erase and undo, then you can do the work you need to do to raise your self-esteem. Low self-esteem is not part of your DNA! When you consider the true nature of who you are, as something that emerged from Universal Power and is connected to Universal Power, the very notion of self-esteem at all is entirely ridiculous! I'm offering but one channel for you to explore when seeking to raise your self-esteem; there are many. I know that subconscious mind reprogramming is the most effective because it cuts right to the core of the emotion behind the cause. You can set yourself free and be your own best friend just by raising your self-esteem. It is that simple. The techniques and methods in this book will show you how to do this.

***

To contact Jim:

Email: info@lutesinternational.com

Websites: www.lutesinternational.com

www.jimluteslive.com

Bill and Cynthia Delaney

Bill and Cynthia Delaney have been mentoring and coaching thousands of people for the past decade. To date, they have spoken to small and large groups more than one thousand times, with crowds of up to 8,000 people, ultimately sharing their messages with well over a hundred thousand people.

After a successful corporate career, Bill founded several aviation companies including a commercial jet trading company in 2003. Cynthia has always been an entrepreneur at heart and has launched numerous business ventures from retail stores to real estate. Over the past eight years, Bill and Cynthia built a $150M Network Marketing Empire with 140,000 people in their organization. They have conducted hundreds of leadership training events and established themselves among the top 1% of leaders in this field.

Cynthia is the founder of www.SelfMadeWoman.com, a women's empowerment organization created to inspire, elevate, and celebrate women's lives and achievements.

Bill and Cynthia have a reputation for being incredibly "authentic" and very "heartfelt." Their ability to inspire Action and Change is widely recognized by the people that attend their events.

The Power of Higher Expectations: Hope is <u>Not</u> Enough

By Bill Delaney

"If you accept the expectations of others, especially negative ones, then you never will change the outcome." ~ Michael Jordan

This quote by the legendary Michael Jordan sounds fundamental, and it is. It is also fundamentally true that we have been influenced by social programming. In life too we may often allow the beliefs, opinions, and expectations of others to influence our results. Let's not be too quick to judge—after all, we once did not know what we do not know. Today is different because today we understand how social programming works and the role it plays in our lives. Today is different. **Today is the day that I'm going to help you establish your expectations and determine your own outcome.**

My expectation in writing this chapter is to help as many people as possible go to the next level in life and the next level and the next level. Always growing and gaining momentum. To help you achieve things you may not "expect." Observe my previous sentence one more time and notice my "intent" and my *expectation.*

I've never accomplished anything by accident. As I look back on my 48 years of life with 20/20 vision, I realize that I never achieved more than I *expected*. Maybe you're the same. Do you ever reflect on your life to see how your expectations impact your outcome? If the answer is NO, I challenge you to complete this chapter, give yourself permission, and spend some time reflecting on the outcomes and the expectations that you had and then apply the lesson you learn to establish new *direction*. I'm not one to live in the past; in fact, I'm a big believer in "mindfulness," yet I do believe that there is great wisdom in learning from the past.

It was 1989 in Waco, Texas, I was engaged to the girl of my dreams and I was very focused on the future. Cynthia and I had big hopes for our future. We knew what we wanted and we had great dreams—visions, if you will, of our future. We did not know how we were going to achieve everything. We simply knew we had to.

I was working as an aircraft mechanic on commercial jet airliners. I was earning $6.30 per hour and at a 40-hour work week I was close to a $200 take home check each week. I thought to myself: how different would my life be if I could just take home $500 per week. That sounded amazing! An expectation set, an extra three hundred dollars a week. I started on my way to make this happen. I worked as much overtime as possible, but it just wasn't enough. I was tired and worn out. I needed a new plan to accomplish my goal of $500 per week, so I looked around and took note of what other people were doing and asked about how much money they were earning. Management and Quality Control were earning what I was hoping for, but they had a decade or more experience than me.

> *To be successful, obsession is required and I was obsessed with achieving my goal; it occupied my mind every minute that I was at work.*

My obsession paid off when a door of opportunity opened. Yes... the people in Quality Control were much older than me, and that meant they had more experience. So how would I overcome this barrier? As Jim Britt stated, "Every income level requires a new you." I couldn't agree more. I saw a crack in the door, a specialized skill called "non-destructive testing" and very few inspectors had this certification. So I enrolled in the closest school I could find, the University of North Texas. A 110-mile drive would challenge me two nights per week for six months. At the age of 20, I became the youngest person in this department where most were twice my age, yet I was not concerned. My expectation was spot on; none of the other people that applied for the position had the certifications that I had so I became the youngest person in the department. My starting wage jumped to $13.80 per hour, which put me right at the edge of my goal.

> *Let's look at my expectations; I expected to take home $500 per week and I did not care that other people thought I was too young or inexperienced. I did not concern myself with their "opinions." My expectation and obsession set me on a path that nearly doubled my income in less than one year!*

This trend has repeated itself several times in my life. Jump to 1999, I set my sights on earning a yearly salary of $60k+ while also moving my wife Cynthia and three-year old son Dillon from Texas to Tucson, Arizona. I had a job earning $64k per year. Shortly after, I realized $64k per year wasn't what I "hoped" it would be. (This is a key; this is where you get your highlighter and start marking.) During a 2014 commencement speech, Jim Carey stated, **"I don't believe in hope. Hope is a beggar. Hope walks through the fire. Faith leaps over it."**

> *Faith, to me, is when expectations are obsessions and all other outcomes will become invisible. Don't hope for an outcome. I cannot remember a single achievement that I "hoped" for. Every great achievement in my life has come through obsessive expectations to absolute realizations. And I have never received more than I expected, not ever!*

Let's head back to 1999, $64k was not the freedom I had dreamed of, so I set a new goal. One that may have seemed a bit ridiculous, but still in the realm of possibility. I decided that doubling my income would be a start and I once again started looking for that open door. Within a few months, I was recruited to be the Vice President of operations for a Tucson-based commercial jet maintenance facility with 570 employees at the ripe old age of 31. Guess what my negotiated salary was… I bet you were close, $134k per year. **This trend has continued on and still holds true today.**

My next ventures were entrepreneurial. I launched several new businesses including management manpower to clients such as DHL Worldwide, aviation component manufacturing, and also commercial jet aircraft sales. *"What? Who sells commercial jets?"* I get that response often when I talk about buying retired Southwest

Airlines aircraft and exporting them to a small airline in another country, but that's another chapter.

Setting higher expectations has certainly played a key role in some of my greatest achievements. It's not the only player, so below are some of the other key principles that I know will help you, as you decide to give yourself permission to achieve your expectations.

1) Don't believe the negative stuff you've been telling yourself, probably most of your life. People get mired down in limiting beliefs based on a single event that happened in their life. Align with an expert to guide you, discover the events holding you back, and break the pattern. One of the best techniques is to realize that the story you've been clinging to is untrue and accept it for what it really is.

2) Others people's expectations and realities are not yours. Just because other people become comfortable being uncomfortable does not mean anything. Set your own expectations and live the life you know you deserve. Most of those who settle will impose settling on you; eliminate their influence.

3) Taking action is the key to achieving expectations. This is where hope comes in. Many people hope for great outcomes and only those that take action will truly succeed. So start doing! It will never appear to be the perfect time, with the perfect plan, with the perfect amount of money, so allow yourself to be perfectly imperfect.

4) Fear is the action killer. Like so many, I too have been frozen in fear many times, but the results were never good. Fear is a player in everyone's life when it's allowed, but we all get to decide how much. So be afraid, and do it anyway. For a great reference on this, check out the TED Talk by Mel Robbins on The 5 Second Rule.

> *FACT: Successful people do the things that unsuccessful people are not willing to do. Successful people think differently and they act differently, which leads me to my next point.*

5) Proximity, this is a big one! Have you ever heard that you become the average of the 5 people that you spend the most time with? Look around at the people you know—what do their lives look like? Look at the lives of the people they hang around. Break away if you don't like what you see. Find a mastermind group to join, even if it's online. Do whatever you have to do to get involved with people who have achieved the lifestyle that you want.

6) Find a mentor or better yet mentors. **This is mission critical!** Many people will make excuses about the cost of coaching or mentorship. If you allow this mindset you might get stuck staring at cost instead of focusing on the value of the outcome. For those of you "money challenged," get innovative, attend free workshops, network, and make new friends. Offer your service to someone in exchange for their mentorship. *Expect it and be obsessed with finding it.*

The next step in achievement is a written Action (Obsession) Plan. Use the outline below to help create yours. Design this to fit you. If money is not your desired outcome, replace it with what is. The point is to have a specific plan.

Guidance, complete these sentences:

I expect to earn $ _____ this year.

Earning $ _____ this year will allow me to _____.

Develop your "Why" (It must evoke emotion in you). There are many great online resources to dig deeper in developing your "Why." I highly recommend the research.

In order to earn $ _____ this year, I will do the following things: _____

(List them out, be specific. List the exact actions that you are willing to do to achieve your desired outcome.)

Jim Carey wrote himself a check for $10 million dollars. A few short years later, he received $10 million dollars for the movie <u>Dumb and Dumber</u>. Now that's what I call the Power of Higher expectation! Vision is key to creating an expectation. Until you see it being a reality, you will block yourself, essentially preventing your own success. And never forget that obsession is a necessity.

Remember my challenge? I bet you can track your personal outcomes to your expectations. It would be a great gift to receive a message from you sharing your story of **"leveling up"** after applying these principles to your life. It has never failed me and I know it will help you too.

Cynthia and I would love to work with you...

IGNITE YOUR DESTINY

By Cynthia Delaney

A couple of years ago, I was talking to a woman that shared her heart, her hardest struggles, the way she dug deep to find her purpose, and how she built upon it in a way that she could give an example to others and leave behind a ripple effect. The ability to strengthen others through life experiences. She expressed how much a purpose-driven life can give you wings you never knew you had. She said, ***"purpose is found through the trial and celebration of life, that which stretches us beyond our perceived limits."*** Once you have found your purpose, your life is driven by a fuel that is unstoppable!

She recalled the trials of her life: losing a young brother in a car accident. Her mom was driving that car, and although not killed in the accident, as a young girl she watched her mom slowly die as she used alcohol to numb the pain. She would hide the vodka bottles to save her mother, but as a young girl, naïve to what addiction and pain are, only rescued by the victim and their fight to be saved, she couldn't make that decision. She fought the pain of watching her mother kill herself behind the quiet, closed doors. Those around her would have never known. She protected her mom from the judgment and kept her family's personal battle to save her a secret. She lost her mom six years after her brother, at only 13 years old, a huge loss in such fragile years, when a daughter needs her mom the most. A family of four became two.

Her dad did his best, raising a teenage daughter alone was a road not traveled. She grew up in an apartment amongst the pain of loss and judged by many on how she lived. She began to notice as people asked, "when are y'all going to have a house? How long have y'all lived like this?" She then realized that not everyone would see her heart, and everyone would instead define her by where she lived.

Many days and nights were spent digging deep to overcome the loss, the pain, the anger, the sadness of her reality, and amongst the diversity, the pages of a warrior were written. *She told me, this is where I decided that only I could define myself! Only I would decide who I would become! Only I would be able to decide what I could accomplish!*

> You can let the world around you define you, or decide to be limited only by your imagination. By what you know you're worth. You can relate to the story of trial, because we have all been there in different ways. You've been tired, beat down, and you've suffered. It's not easy sharing our vulnerabilities, our struggles. But, you are amazing! You are beautiful! You are strong! And your stories need to be told!

I'm going to share the woman's name, because she gave me permission. She said, *"It's time I shared the struggles, so I can help others through their own."* **This woman is me!**

I'm saying I am strong and you are too. I'm saying be brave, dig deep. I'm saying be all who you were made to be. I'm going to teach you how to be brave, to dig deep, and to be Victorious!

You may be asking the question "why did I choose to fight so hard, through the frustration and the struggles?" Well, the answer is that the options scared me more than the fight! **I had a larger Fear of Fear.** The Fear that scared me most was not living life, or watching it pass me by! I dug deep and drew from the experiences I did not want to repeat.

I remember being in furniture sales—the problem was that it was my own furniture! I remember pawning our personal possessions to pay our bills and the feeling of filing for bankruptcy and losing our house. I thought of the example of a car traveling down the road and getting a flat tire, pulling to the side of the road and looking at that flat tire, then slashing the other three just because the one didn't work. I decided to move on. I would take on the moments that looked like a barrier and defeat them! I had to define myself as a fighter or decide to submit! I chose to fight! And it was worth it! No amount of uncomfortable would be more painful than watching my family struggle.

I am no longer the woman I was. I decided who I wanted to be and started taking steps toward her because of believing I was worthy. *You define yourself, your strength, your focus, and your passion! What is your passion? You and I are the same. You are reading this because you want more for your family and others around you. You want to LIVE not exist! Right?*

Time is our most precious commodity. It's not about being perfect! It's about owning who you know you can be, who you want to be as a person, and learning along the way! **Dare to believe you can achieve anything! Because you can!**

I don't want you to think for one second that it's easy. I want you to know it's worth it.

I look back on the trials and being down on my knees, moments of being frozen by the loss of motion due to the battering that life can bring. The kind that severs your nerves needed to feel, to function. We can all see where there were times in our lives where we felt lost or abandoned, even by those who loved us most! We can remember the crying, the punching a wall or a pillow, slamming a door. Wanting to run away, to yell at someone. Mainly to know that someone was listening, or that someone gave a flying flip.

Looking back on life's curveballs, hard hits, and slaps in the gut, no one ever could give me the hand I needed. Some tried. I heard, "pray and it will fall out of the sky when the time is right." And "take the time you need. You'll figure it out." That was others making themselves feel better because they gave me some advice that they felt at the end of the day they accomplished something, much like a check list. Like they did their part not even knowing if I slit my wrists the next day, because they didn't call to check in or follow up, sometimes for days or weeks, with no attachment to anything but themselves. Check, they did their part!

I realize there has been one and only one person who has come to my rescue. One person that has made the calls that would talk me off the cliff! That would understand the inner strength to pull from and push me hard enough to make or break me. To bring out the fighter, to give me no excuses. To take me to the place of worthiness for happiness, success, and for purpose. We are all given choice. My choice to listen to this person in my life allowed me to be mindful of God's greatest gift of life to all of us!

> Choice! The choice to be, do, and give anything, because it must start with you! We all decide our fate. However long, however strong! However loud or purposeful to the world!

I write this on a day where after all my victories against the odds, after the haters who tried to distract me and ruin my legacy, after all the trials that I have come out of victorious, I am still flesh and blood. I can be wounded on the battlefield of Life! I can be thrown down hard and have the wind knocked out of me! I can feel defeated!

Time is precious and every day I wake up thanking God for all that we must be grateful for. I lead my life with positivity and I'm attracted to the lights that shine bright, the laughter, and all those who give to others! Those of truth, transparency, and a giving heart!

My goal is for you to run to your friends, and let them know you have answers! So they too can benefit from the storms they have weathered and lessons they have learned. I want to know I made a difference, and that I wasn't starving yet instead sharing in the abundance while empowering the hungry. They win, you win, we all win! *One man or woman can only do the lifting of one man and one woman, but many moving together has and will continue to move mountains.*

This is about creating abundance; this is about YOU. I don't take that lightly. Helping others become empowered and live in abundance has become our legacy. Proactive living! I'm being as real as they come. If you see any shame in that, then quite frankly you're not the no-settle person, **winners fight, fighters win**, failure-is-not-an-option person looking for real answers and no BS that I wrote this for. ***But I believe you are. In fact, I know you are!***

Everyone wants abundance, love, finances, experiences, and everyone can have it, but only those that believe it will happen for them will experience it! If you believe you can or you believe you can't, you're right! Thoughts are absolutely things and you will only be able to attain that which you can imagine.

This is where your story begins. So let's get started with this! What you think you deserve will set the bar to the maximum amount the universe will allow you. Notice I said you, not the universe. The universe has given you an unlimited amount of possibility and choice. So will you live in a mindset of lack, or a mindset of abundance?

On the other side of fear, there is always freedom! How do you know if you just kind of want it? That is the big question because you either do or you don't. You might say you want it, but you just kind of want it. You can tell because when it's time to cheat, you give in. When it stops being easy, you give up. As soon as things get uncomfortable, you go searching for something easier. If there is an acceptable excuse, you take it the easy way. You stop at good enough, and level off when it seems reasonable. You get sucked into cheats, hacks, and shortcuts when the biggest shortcut of all is hours and hours of unnoticed and under-appreciated work. This is what most people do and when you do what most people do, you get what most people get!

NOW is the moment you get the chance for separation. The moment when you decide to keep going and not give up, you create distance between yourself and average! HOW BAD DO YOU WANT IT?!

***

To Contact Bill and Cynthia:

www.BillandCynthiaDelaney.com

Email: Admin@BillandCynthiaDelaney.com

www.SelfMadeWoman.com

www.Facebook.com/BillDelaneyOnline

www.Facebook.com/CynthiaDelaneyOnline

www.Facebook.com/BillandCynthiaDelaney

www.Facebook.com/SelfMadeWoman4u

Alison Lalieu

Alison Lalieu is an experienced Neuroleadership Coach with hundreds of hours of Coaching experience. As CEO of UBalancer Solutions (a national network of Coaches making a difference though their work in Education, Business, and Sport), Alison brings a vision to create the best Coaching network globally. She feels a strong desire to make a difference to the lives of her clients, as together they explore and create a roadmap for personal and professional change, designing leadership surfboards. Neuroleadership Coaching is exciting as it helps people better understand how their brain is key to unlocking their motivation, innovation, and performance, and Alison believes that blending this with Emotional Intelligence and Life Balance Coaching supports clients in a holistic way. Her hope is for people to thrive in an ever-changing world, and she feels privileged to be in a position to inspire people to unlock their full potential.

Alison loves her family, spending time with friends, and traveling. She is a lifelong learner and loves connecting with people who share her vision for leaving the world a better place. One conversation at a time, and through the magic of our collective effort, we can create a well-being revolution.

UBalancer Solutions

By Alison Lalieu

Ignite the Leader in You

There seems to be a Global change energy in the air with volatility, uncertainty, and complexity becoming the norm. With the electric pace of research across all of the sciences, many of us find ourselves reeling with a fountain of new knowledge flooding our smart devices and our lives daily. People working in 2025 may look back on today's working life with disbelief as their days play out so differently. Information now turns over every couple of years, leaving educational institutions wondering how they can keep their courses relevant. Over the next 20 years, we will experience as much change in the way we work as we did in the previous 2,000 years, and guaranteed jobs will seem a distant memory as the average person experiences multiple career changes. With 50 billion devices expected to be connected to the internet by 2020, and automation, robotics, and 3- D printing reshaping the face of education, business, security, production, medicine, and the way we run our homes, another industrial revolution is rolling in.

Around the world, people are increasingly accessing the internet, an extraordinary gateway to the possibility and hope that springs from this unlimited pool of new knowledge. Along with this positive access also comes graphic exposure to the challenges faced by so many—poverty, displacement, lack of a quality education, crime, wars, and acts of terror. Vivid images of people whose lives have been shattered cross our news screens, our Twitter feeds, and other social media outlets minute by minute, shaking up our belief system as to what we feel is safe and certain in our world.

Roaming the savannas, our ancestors had brains that were wired to detect threat, alerting them to potential attacks by roaming sable toothed tigers! Over time, humans began living together in tribes (safety in numbers) and enjoying the benefits that came from looking out for each other. The idea that 'I could have a nap if someone else is watching out for me' came into play. Over the millennia, our tribes have grown into villages, towns, cities, and mega-cities, and thanks to the miracle of neuroplasticity, our brains have rewired over time to adapt to new living environments. What hasn't changed, though, is that our tendency to detect a threat remains much more powerful than our tendency to assume everything is OK. So when our world starts feeling uncertain, our natural instinct is to withdraw and to fear what is coming our way.

According to neuroscience, there are two main organizing principles of our human brain; we like to feel safe and we like to feel certain. When we experience a loss of control and unexpected and unexplained things start to happen regularly, the limbic part of our brain fires up and prepares us for the proverbial 3 F's 'fight, flight, or flee.' And that's exactly what we see playing out across the world at the moment in a political sense, where people are voting to return to a time when things may have felt easier and less threatening.

The world is crying out for Leadership, not only from within political ranks, but from each and every one of us, within our homes, our tribes, and our workplaces. It's a special brand of Leadership that the world is now craving, a kind of personal entrepreneurship that empowers us to ride the waves of change with agility and speed, whilst staying mindful, calm, and reassured that change is a good thing.

It feels like we're on a surfboard with huge waves of change washing up towards us, one rolling in after another. I see that we have three options: do nothing and allow the waves to crash on us and wash us up somewhere down the shore; or take a deep breath and dive into the waves, hoping they will pass over and we can resurface undamaged but still stuck in the same spot. It's the third option that really excites me. What if we are able to design our own personal entrepreneurial surfboard, with all the flexibility, agility, and the speed we need to ride these waves of change and experience the thrill, wherever it may take us?

With this surfboard, a fast-paced world of change would no longer feel threatening. It could even become something we long for, providing us with opportunities and the chance to start over or stand out from the crowd. I dream of a time when our brain may rewire to a point where change represents safety and certainty, and nothing to withdraw from or feel afraid of.

One of the many blessings in my Coaching career has been the chance to grasp every learning opportunity and design my own Leadership surfboard along the way. Part of my journey has taken me to the villa of a Global entrepreneur, whose mission is to empower every person to find their natural flow and grow their entrepreneurial spirit. His passion comes from a deep belief that every person should band together to help the world solve its problems to make the Global goals set by the United Nations for 2030 become a reality. Imagine a world of no poverty, zero hunger, good health and well-being, quality education for all, gender equality, clean water and sanitation, affordable and clean energy, decent work and economic goals, industry and innovation and infrastructure, reduced inequalities and sustainable cities and communities. Sounds like change worthy of our energy and attention. As governments alone can't do it, I too am on a mission to ignite a fire within every person so that they can jump on their surfboards and start to make a difference in even just one of these Global areas.

It's about inspiring and empowering the Leaders of tomorrow, today, as they get in touch with their own Life Purpose, the stamp they want to imprint on these Global challenges and the legacy they want to leave behind within their families, tribes, and workplaces. Every one of you is a Leader. Are you ready for the ride?

As you read this, I urge you to start thinking about your own entrepreneurial surfboard and how you're going to shape it so that you can prepare yourself and look ahead with excitement, inspired to grasp the future with both hands. They say there is no time like the present, so let's take the first step to feeling empowered to embrace a wild ride as you craft your own Leadership style, of a kind that the world is now demanding.

The foundation level of surfboard construction involves taking the time to really get to Know Yourself.

Gone are the days of studying subjects and courses that someone else thought might suit you. Tapping into the wealth of talent and personality profiling tools available will guide your understanding of what kind of work will keep you motivated and enthusiastic. Will your Leadership grow with you working in an innovative creative environment, or perhaps is your niche more people focused? Are you great at providing services, or perhaps your Leadership will shine when you're given the chance to manage backend systems, data, and processes?

As you keep designing your surfboard, I encourage you to get in touch with your top five Values in life. Those deep core principles that you live by, that inform your everyday decisions, and provide a firm foundation in times of change and uncertainty. I'd love to share mine with you— they are being Authentic (genuine with every person I meet), Transparent (honest and open in my communication), showing Respect at all times, staying Curious in every situation, and living in a way that people can Trust me for my word and my actions. Over the years, I have grown to trust this part of my Leadership surfboard because it rarely lets me down. When the waves start breaking around me in a different way, I reflect on my top five Values and the board just carves into the wave at a different angle.

The next part of the surfboard is a true connection with your Character Strengths. What are you really good at and how do you know? When you access your Strengths daily, how are you able to influence your own and others' paths? Focusing on your Strengths in a deliberate action each day brings untold rewards, especially in relation to how positive you feel and the contribution you are making. Gratitude is a Strength of mine, and I make a point of journaling every night, recalling how thankful I am for one good thing that happened in my day. I even go so far as to write how grateful I am for something wonderful that is going to happen the next day, imagining that it has already happened and turned out to be amazing! I believe that everyone I have ever met and every life experience I have ever had has brought me to a point where the universe will deliver when the timing is right. The law of attraction holds true.

It is so exciting to see your entrepreneurial Leadership surfboard starting to really take shape as you enter the Change phase. Imagine a caterpillar entering its cocoon, a place teeming with activity. Within this space swirls a chemical soup of change, reforming the cellular mix as a stunningly beautiful butterfly is created. Change can be difficult because it often involves the pain of uncertainty, yet without change we may not unlock all of our potential. Just like that butterfly, once we emerge with vibrant wings, who knows where the ride will take us?

I believe that one of the missing links in this space is self-awareness around our Emotional Intelligence, our capacity to be smarter with our feelings, being able to read emotions as important information and recognize our emotional and behavioral patterns and how well they serve us. The way in which we navigate our way through our emotions and those of others guides how we respond in life to changes that comes our way.

Are we able to get off autopilot, take a few deep breaths, process the information that our emotions have provided, and respond in a calm, respectful way?

In the Emotionally Intelligent part of our surfboard, Optimism plays a major part. A blend of possibility and hope, Optimism creates Leaders who can thrive in a world that is anything but certain, a Leader who can recognize opportunity, move fast, and learn from mistakes whilst crafting new solutions in a dynamic and exciting way, paving the way for meaningful and dynamic change.

Future Leadership surfboards will demand Leaders who show Empathy to others and appreciate the flexibility and compassion that encourages thriving teams. The Leader of the future will also succeed by understanding the importance of Empathy to self, especially in the realm of Life Balance. A state of overwhelm with multiple demands and not enough hours in their day is likely to be the norm, and an appreciation that Life Balance comes from feeling in control of the choices we are making is helpful. When things feel out of our control, being able to adjust to our new circumstances quickly enables us to ride the waves more fluidly.

Hundreds of hours of Coaching in this space leads me to share a few Life Balance tips with you. Build diversity into your life, make sure you do at least fifteen minutes every day of something you love, and think carefully about your Values and what's important to you. Honor your priorities mindfully each and every day as life is short and in the end, it's the memories of the people we love and how we spent our time with them that will be remembered. Seek experiential adventures, and get to know people from cultures other than your own. Prioritize a digital free day every so often and listen to connect mindfully, aware that successful multitasking is a myth much of the time.

There is a very special Mindful spot on the Leadership surfboard of tomorrow. It is a space where we slow down, get off autopilot, breathe deeply, and notice our thoughts without judgement. A sanctuary we can access any time of the day, simply by leaning in and remembering to let go of some of the fifty to seventy thoughts that clutter our brain daily and steal our clarity of thought and creativity. Quiet times like these also enable us to connect with that greater life question, our 'why'!

And so I ask you this very important question: "How do you want to be remembered by your family, your friends, and your colleagues?" Imagine it's your 80th birthday, and your adult child is standing up making a speech about your life. What is it that you would like to hear them say… touching your heart and making you think it had all been worthwhile? These are the big Life Purpose questions that bring so much more passion, energy, meaning, and vision to our lives. No matter how the waves of change thrash us about, aligning with our Purpose keeps us on track to our greater vision, like a True North Star.

I hope you're still with me, and in your mind crafting the most amazing personal Leadership surfboard you've ever imagined!

Another powerful piece in the puzzle is having an understanding of the Neuroscience of how the brains works so that you can hone your Leadership, greatly improving your impact as you begin to better understand how people think and communicate. Leaders who understand how other people's brains respond when we interact with them can use this powerful knowledge to motivate and engage, influence, manage, and inspire.

It's time for you to pull it all together, to split open the cocoon and give back to your world in creative ways you never dreamed possible. You're entering a liberating, exciting, flexible, dynamic, creative, fast-paced, happy, and thrilling world.

It's You, and a chance to craft your own personal brand, whilst embracing the power of the world that you now live in. Yes, it's volatile, uncertain, and very complex, but wow, it's a maze of opportunity, has unprecedented potential for collaboration and enterprise on a scale never seen before. Now is the time for you to learn everything you can about Thought Leaders in spheres of your interest. Follow them on social media, sign up to their promotions, and join their networks. Find Mentors and devour every word they say, whilst develop a daily habit of reading motivational books and quotes to inspire you.

As a part of designing your brand, reflect back on your natural Talents, your Values, and Character Strengths. Build them into your story, and let the world know what you're about. I believe that we are all here to make a difference, and contribute in some way to leaving the world a better place than we found it. To find our personal entrepreneurial edge, with our contribution aligned with our Values and Life Purpose, enabling us to surf the waves of change with ease and contribute to the Global goals in our own unique way.

Some of us may find stable permanent jobs, yet this is unlikely to be the norm in years to come. The faster the pace of technology and the more it impacts our lives, the greater will be our need to create our own employment and networks; to skill up, design our own surfboard, and start surfing! I recently met a young 10-year-old boy who was writing a series of children's books and self-publishing, whilst also having fun blogging weekly. His surfboard is coming along famously!

There is something very powerful about taking control of our own story that resonates within all of us. The world is an exciting place, especially now that the internet can be a force to connect and unite us. Whatever position you find yourself in, I encourage you to do some 'heart work,' to think more about your dream. You are an inspiration, you are unique, and you are in a position to exert a positive influence on the people in your world on a daily basis.

Use your Leadership style to positively impact the world, one conversation at a time. Feel proud that you have invested energy into finding out what's important to you, what you love about yourself, and what you now want to bring to the world. To those of you with a vision of making a global difference, I say to you 'anything is possible.' You just have to believe it!

The final piece of the surfboard is the Investing in Yourself piece. Sign up for every relevant course, network with like-minded people, write proposals, and source funding for your ideas. Remember that it is only through being true to self that you can create the personal Leadership you are going to need to survive and thrive. Anything is possible for you if you believe in yourself enough, and know that you deserve the best in life.

In my own personal journey in the past few years, I have ridden many waves of change and throughout it all have been gradually building my personal Leadership surfboard. My hope is for you to get started and not waste a day! As sure as the world keeps turning, the pace of change will keep churning. There is no turning back the clock to a bygone era, and we all have a collective part to play in leading not only ourselves, but in responsibly creating a sustainable future for us all.

Change brings opportunity, and ours here is to motivate, inspire, and prepare the Leaders of tomorrow, today. To feel empowered to rise to the challenge, to be brave and risk losing what hasn't worked well in the past; to lead by example and promote our vision whilst growing the skills essential so that we have the most exciting surfboard.

No matter how much the world changes, each one of us is a Leader, and those we lead will thrive as they witness our surfboard carving flow through the waves.

I wish you happiness and success as you Ignite the Leader in You.

***

To Contact Alison:

Mobile: +61 413 997 495

Email: alison@ubalancer.com.au

Web: www.ubalancer.com.au

Facebook: www.facebook.com/UBalancer

Twitter: www.twitter.com/UBalancer

Skype: alalieu

Andrea Wilson Woods

Andrea Wilson Woods is an ICF Associate Certified Coach who specializes in career and business coaching; a writer who loves to tell stories; and a patient advocate who runs a nonprofit. Forever a Steel Magnolia, Andrea returned to Birmingham, Alabama, after living her entire adult life in Los Angeles. The following year, she founded her coaching and consulting company Build Your BLISSS (BYB). Andrea believes through BYB's practical methods and the power of storytelling that people can create joyful, passionate, and authentic lives. Andrea obtained her master's degree in professional writing from the University of Southern California, and her nonfiction writing has won national awards. In 2002, Andrea founded **Blue Faery: The Adrienne Wilson Liver Cancer Association** after losing her 15-year-old sister Adrienne, whom she raised for seven years, to stage IV liver cancer. Raising Adrienne has been Andrea's greatest joy in life; losing Adrienne to primary liver cancer has been her greatest loss. Andrea started Blue Faery because she doesn't want another person to lose a loved one to liver cancer, and she wants the world to know Adrienne's spirit, strength, and courage. Andrea plans to publish her memoir in 2017.

Better Off Dead
How One Fatalistic Thought Forced Me to Face My Fear of Change

By Andrea Wilson Woods

I was standing in the kitchen of the house my husband and I had rented for over 10 years. We lived in Burbank, California, a Los Angeles suburb nestled in the heart of the city between Hollywood, Glendale, and the San Fernando Valley. With one of the best public school districts in the state, Burbank was one of the safest and most expensive places to live in LA. We could not afford to buy a home in the neighborhood that we loved.

Our little blue house on Valley Street was built in 1948. Though the management company had replaced the linoleum, the rest of the kitchen was in its original state. I ran my fingers over the blue-tiled countertop. No matter how hard I scrubbed with a toothbrush, I could never clean the grout. I waited as the coffeemaker whirred and crunched as it grinded the beans. I hated our coffeemaker. It was too expensive, too loud, too difficult to clean, but my husband had insisted we buy it. He liked fresh beans every day. I couldn't tell the difference. Then again, I only drink coffee for the caffeine. I don't like the taste.

Though it was mid-morning and I was inside our air-conditioned house, the dry heat of late August crept into my bones. I used to like the weather in Southern California, but it never changes. I wiped my left nostril with my finger and saw once again that my nose was bleeding. I have dry skin, dry hair, and dry nasal passages. That summer, my body went to war with the weather.

I washed my hands. I poured some coffee. I stared at that blue tile. That 1948-impossible-to-clean blue tile. As I grabbed my cup, I thought to myself ... *I would be better off dead*. Almost as quickly as the thought entered my mind, I dismissed it. I knew I wouldn't be better off dead. I didn't want to die. Not anymore. I had not wished for death in 10 years.

***

When I was 22 years old, I gained custody of my eight-year-old sister Adrienne. I raised her for almost seven years in Los Angeles. One month after her 15th birthday, she came home from high school saying she couldn't breathe. Six hours later, an ER doctor told us Adrienne had tumors in her liver and lungs. Two days later, she was diagnosed with primary liver cancer. In less than five months, Adrienne died. At home. In our little blue house on Valley Street.

I lost my child, my sister, and my best friend. Part of me died with Adrienne, leaving a void so vast that nothing could fill it. I was 29 years old, and the most important person in my life was gone. Though I pretended I was doing okay, I was never okay. For several years, I wanted to die. I didn't wear a seatbelt when I drove by myself because I hoped I would get into a fatal car accident. I know how irrational it sounds now, but it made sense at the time. Of course, nothing happened. Not so much as a fender bender. One day, I realized how ridiculous I was being and started wearing my seatbelt again. However, my attitude didn't change. I missed Adrienne so much I wanted to die. I knew how I would do it, and it would have been easy. I concocted a detailed suicide plan, but aborted it after my boyfriend found out. He had helped me raise Adrienne. She will hate you if you kill yourself he said. He was right so I did not end my life. The will went away, but the desire did not.

During the summer of 2004, almost three years after Adrienne's death, I was in a plane flying from Boston to LA. The first half of the flight was unremarkable. Then, we flew into a storm. Hitting turbulence is one thing; being shaken up and down like salt grains in a shaker is a different experience. The captain instructed us to return to our seats immediately. The flight attendants told us to fasten our seatbelts before they scurried to their seats. Parents held their children. Other passengers grasped their armrests until their knuckles turned white. After minutes of bobbing up and down, passengers began holding hands. We were in this thing together. I heard few sounds except our carry-on luggage banging over our heads and sliding under our feet. There was an occasional scream, but mostly silence punctured by cries of babies. I reminded myself I loved roller coasters and this was one long roller coaster ride. Unfortunately, I had the window seat. I could see the storm lashing out as if Mother Nature didn't want us in her domain. I slid the cover over the window. I prayed. *I want to live. I want to live.* About an hour later, the ride ended and everyone cheered. We landed at LAX shortly thereafter. When I saw the sidewalk outside of baggage claim, I kissed it. I had never been happier to see that nasty, grey concrete in all my life. After that horrific flight, I never thought about suicide again. No matter how much I missed Adrienne, I wanted to live.

I don't think you ever get over a loss. As time passes, you learn to live with the hole in your heart. My boyfriend and I ended our relationship; Adrienne's death ripped us apart. I refused to leave the house where my little girl died. I met my husband. He dated me, moved in with me, and proposed to me. We married in September 2006. I quit acting and teaching, the two careers I had when I was raising Adrienne. I went to graduate school and obtained my master's degree in writing. I embarked on several career paths: professor, research analyst, fundraiser, writer, social media manager, etc. Also, I founded Blue Faery: The Adrienne Wilson Liver Cancer Association, a nonprofit dedicated to fighting primary liver cancer. I was determined to make sure what happened to Adrienne didn't happen to anyone else. No one deserves liver cancer.

***

Now here I was—10 years later—sitting at my kitchen table thinking about being dead. Why did I have that thought? Yes, I was frustrated, unhappy, and tired, but my life wasn't terrible. Next month, my husband and I would celebrate our eight-year wedding anniversary. However, we had been having problems for four years. We had begun therapy about two years ago. We did couples counseling. We did individual counseling. We went to psychiatrists, psychologists, and marriage and family therapists. Though he felt like I had given up, I felt like we had given it our all. No one can say we didn't try. We were two of the most persistent people I knew.

We were no longer doing therapy together, but he had found a therapist for himself. To me, our problems seemed unfixable.

The previous summer, I had completed a 300-hour yoga teacher training. I didn't want to become a yoga teacher; in fact, I was the only person in the training who wasn't a yoga teacher. I wanted to deepen my practice and understanding of the philosophy. One of the many techniques I had learned was how to write a bhavana. A bhavana is an emotionally charged visualization that is positive, concrete, and specific. By writing a bhavana, you are remembering the future.

Since Adrienne had died, I had flitted from one career to the next because I have always been good at landing jobs. I knew how to find them, how to write a resume, how to rock an interview, and how to use LinkedIn. My freelance writing business consisted mostly of resume-writing clients. I didn't take a salary as the founder of my nonprofit, so I needed a 'real' job. The year before, I had written a career bhavana with the following components:

- Uses my talents including writing, marketing, social media, teaching, people skills
- Within 10 miles of Burbank
- Pays a minimum of $60K but ideally $65K or higher with full benefits
- Happy engaging coworkers
- Must feel as though I'm making a difference in the world

A few months after writing down what I wanted, I received a call for my first interview with a national nonprofit. After several months of interviews, I began working for them in February 2014. I was thrilled because the job hit every bullet point in my career bhavana. After a strong 90-day review and a 10-percent raise, they fired me on my 100th day. Fired!?! I had never been fired in my life. I didn't see it coming. I had found what I thought was my dream job, and I was fired. Talk about a bitch slap from the universe.

That same spring, I was working with an editor on my book, which had been the thesis for my master's degree. He said my memoir about raising Adrienne and losing her to cancer was the best book he had ever edited in his career. He said he gave my book to a well-known editor at Doubleday. He even asked me to work for him. We negotiated a salary with an anticipated start day of early September. After I sent him the final payment for his editing services, he disappeared. Poof! Vanished. Despite many emails and phone calls, I never heard from him again.

I felt like a hamster running on an exercise wheel. I wasn't going anywhere. I had not gone anywhere. Somehow, I was moving yet I was stuck between who I was, who I wanted to be, and who I was destined to be. I went to our bedroom and found my embroidered-butterfly tote bag that I had used during my yoga training. All my journals were still in there. I began looking over my notes. I stopped at the page titled kriya yoga.

"The definition of insanity is doing the same thing over and over and expecting different results." – Albert Einstein

Kriya yoga is the yoga of action, and there are three steps.

1. Tapas: means to generate heat. To generate 'heat' you must take a deliberate, contrary action.
2. Svadhyaya: means to study yourself and the results of your actions.
3. Ishvarapranidhana: means to surrender the results to god/spirit/universe.

Kriya yoga is like the serenity prayer. God, grant me the serenity to accept the things I cannot change (ishvarapranidhana), the courage to change the things I can (tapas), and the wisdom to know the difference (svadhyaya). Another way to remember it is to refine your action, reflect on it, and release the results.

I stared at my notes. I continued to sip my coffee. I thought about the concept of change. When I was a little girl, I wanted to be taller, so I would hang from our swing set for as long as possible. This exercise did not lengthen my body though it did lead to sore arms. As children we are eager to grow up as quickly as possible, and in order to grow, our bodies must change.

- Fact: If our bodies don't change, we don't grow.
- If we don't fear physical change, why do we fear mental, emotional, and spiritual changes?
- How do we go from being fearless, eager children to fearful, reluctant adults?
- How did I go from being a fearless, enthusiastic girl to a fearful, unhappy woman?

What we fail to realize or refuse to acknowledge is **to grow mentally, emotionally, and spiritually, our mindsets must change.** We must face our fears including the biggest fear of all: change.

When I was a graduate teaching assistant, I worked for an anthropology professor. He taught me scientists are always rethinking their theories of evolution as more fossils are discovered. Yet, one thing is certain: humans are the most adaptable species on earth. So why is it that we can adapt yet refuse to change?

Looking back, from the day I took Adrienne to the ER to the day she died, every moment was different. We lived in a constant state of change. Yet, we figured it out as we went along because we had no other choice. Cancer forces you to adapt, to pivot, to adjust, to change. So, I knew as much as I hated and feared change, I was capable of changing my life. But I wasn't ready.

***

September – December 2014

The following month I attended a medical conference in San Francisco. I stayed with one of my best friends. After the conference was over, I went out back to his place. I don't know what made me burst into tears, but once I started crying, I couldn't stop. Being a bachelor, he didn't have any tissues. I blew my nose so many times he ran out of toilet paper. I remember murmuring "I'll never find my Rhett Butler in Los Angeles." He replied, "no, you won't."

The following weekend, my husband took me to see my favorite movie, *Gone With The Wind,* on the big screen. As we were walking back to his car, he was talking, but I wasn't listening. I kept thinking how long I had wanted to leave Los Angeles. The only reason I had stayed was for him. I had written numerous blog posts including a four-part series titled *Learning to Love LA Again* because I wanted to love the city of angels again. I wanted to love the city where I had raised Adrienne, where I had buried Adrienne, and where I had created many fond memories with her. I never thought I would leave our little blue house on Valley Street where Adrienne died. But before my husband and I reached his car, I was ready to leave Los Angeles.

Once I made the decision, I couldn't stop smiling. I had lived in Los Angeles for 24 years—my entire adult life. I had lived in Burbank for 17 of those years. I had lived in the same house for 13 years. Yet, **I was ready to take a different action**. I had no plan. I had no job. I had no idea where I was going, but it didn't matter. I knew the journey was more important than the destination. I trusted the universe had my back.

I told my husband. He never tried to talk me out of it, which was odd but a relief. Maybe he sensed that he couldn't stop me. With or without his support, I was leaving Los Angeles. I looked at a map and noted all the cities where I had friends/family. I knew people from as far northwest as Washington state to as far east as Washington, D.C. I narrowed my options to the southeast because all my family lives in that part of the country. I decided on Birmingham because I went to high school there. I knew people and knew the city. Plus, the cost of living is far less in Alabama than in California.

The next eight weeks became a nonstop whirlwind of preparing to move my husband into an apartment in Los Angeles and me into an apartment in Birmingham. The move forced us to go through all our stuff. What we didn't sell on Craigslist or donate to charities, we gave away or threw in the trash. As someone who loves to scrapbook, I keep every birthday card, every letter, etc. But mementos take up space. I was going from a four bedroom, two-bath house with a garage to a two bedroom, one-bath apartment with no parking. I didn't have room for excess stuff. Though I kept

Adrienne's journals and most of her artwork, I threw away years of paper memories. I never knew letting go of the past would feel so good.

***

January 2015 – present

One month after arriving in Birmingham, a new client found me on LinkedIn. He made me realize how much value I give my clients. In our last conversation, he thanked me for reminding me of the man he was. In our short time working together, his self-esteem had returned. I understood my true calling went far beyond resume writing. I needed to change my business model and become serious about who I am and what I do.

Within weeks, I began an intense 10-month, holistic life, career, and executive coaching program. I finished the program in December 2015. The following month, I passed the International Coach Federation exam to become an Associate Certified Coach. I started my business Build Your BLISSS LLC. Since January, I have created two live workshop series, a VIP Intensive program, and monthly coaching packages. Though I focus on career and business coaching, **the fear of change permeates people's lives**. I use kriya yoga, bhavana, and other practical methods including storytelling in my Build Your BLISSS business. Our mission is to help people create joyful, passionate, and authentic lives so they will become role models for themselves, their loved ones, and their communities.

I thank the universe for that moment in my kitchen when I thought I was better off dead. I needed to have that fatalistic thought to overcome my inertia and face my fear of change. Though I don't recommend such drastic steps to my clients, I needed to move 2000 miles. I needed to divorce my husband. I needed to live alone. I needed to trust my gut. I needed to learn to love and accept myself for who I am. I needed all those things to happen to understand why I am here.

For the first time since my sister Adrienne died, I know what I am supposed to do with the rest of my life. Coach amazing clients, write incredible stories, and advocate for liver cancer patients.

***

Andrea offers free 30-minute consultations for her VIP Intensive and monthly coaching packages. You may book an appointment at https://calendly.com/andrea-wilson-woods/30min-free-consultation

You may also contact Andrea via:

Email: blisss@andreawilsonwoods.com

Website: www.andreawilsonwoods.com

Facebook: https://www.facebook.com/AuthorAndreaWilsonWoods/

LinkedIn: https://www.linkedin.com/in/andreawilsonwoods

Twitter: https://twitter.com/andreawilwoods

Bill Leydic

William (Bill) Leydic is an entrepreneur specializing in Health and Fitness. He is an International Speaker, touching the lives of hundreds of thousands through his own determination to overcome illness, exhaustion, and many of his own health issues. Bill teaches the importance of being in touch with your mind, body, and soul.

Bill started a career as "punk rocker" in the 1980s, allowing him to travel the world and play on many stages, preparing him for future endeavors. He is gifted in many ways. Through his own life experiences, Bill is well known as 'Bill the Relic Hunter' in the series Time Searches. His ability to communicate with Civil War soldiers continues his long-time family history of relic hunting.

Bill continues his ventures as an engineer by trade, and as he continues with his venture Time Searchers, he has mastered a balance with health and fitness. He is a Personal Development Coach, Health and Fitness Instructor/Coach, and Speaker. Of the many lives Bill has touched throughout the years, his peers, clients, and friends will tell you he will always go the "extra mile" and out of his way to help others grow in all aspects of their lives.

Reflecting on Your Reflection
A Wake-up Call to Health and Fitness

By Bill Leydic

To change your reflection, you must first change your mind. Easier said than done at times, or is it? Have you ever walked past a window and caught your own reflection and didn't recognize who was staring back at you? Or possibly caught your reflection, thinking you're being followed, and it was just all that extra stuff you carry around with you on a daily basis? I have, and it was a major wake up in my life! I'm here to share my journey, my wake-up call in life, with first deciding to decide.

My health had suffered for many years. I was intellectually aware from the doctor visits and medications; practically, I wasn't doing anything to create a healthy alternative lifestyle... yet. I knew I needed to make a change and most of my life I was not committed to doing the work. The self-chatter in my head was holding on to all the problems I was facing at the time and making excuses. I'm an engineer by trade, and an entrepreneur, already at odds in a world where two careers seldom cross paths. I have always been a risk taker and with my intuition, sixth sense, and a couple out of body experiences, adventure has long been a part of my life. I have been a relic hunter for many years and found my share of great relics/artifacts. My business partner and I created a series called Time Searchers. I find it somewhat humorous I have been running a business called Time Searchers, yet running out of time towards my health and fitness.

I have been overwhelmed by high blood pressure, high cholesterol, kidney stones, surgery from stones, back pain, knee issues, fatty liver, and the list goes on, and all which this implies—poor sleeping, mood changes, hair loss, aggravation, lack of focus in all areas of life. Including trying to fit in my relic hunting that I love so much and build a business, and have loving relationships at this level=burnout! We often hit a low point in life, not understanding this may be a wake-up call. Sometimes it is and sometimes you go a little further down before hitting the bottom. Have you ever caught yourself repeating what you need to do and just have not got up to do it?

Now what you say to yourself is of the utmost importance! Now is when you decide if you will continue down this spiral and bring on premature death or illness, or change the course. I made the decision to change the course. I took a long look in the mirror at my reflection. This is not easy—it is necessary. And I will tell you that for me in the end, it was worth it. You now get to decide. Do you love the person looking back at you? Are you ready to now dig deeper than ever before and change the course on which you are spiraling? I decided YES, I was ready. I was ready to become the best me I could possibly become and set out to take the steps necessary to break this cycle.

The steps I began to take have now led me in a direction I once only dreamed was possible. As I grew into the person I am today—a Public Speaker and Authority on Health and Nutrition, a Marathon Athlete—I Coach others with the same methods I used, and I will encourage you to do the same. This is my reflection of my reflection. I learned to love myself healthy and fit... it starts with one step.

EXERCISE

Begin walking, swimming, dancing, moving... begin. Make the decision that you love you enough to be physically strong and add years to your life, not for anyone else, just for yourself and the rest will follow. I chose to walk. Pick something you enjoy and do a little every day. Set small obtainable goals so you don't let yourself down. Each day push a little bit more and get more and more comfortable with activity. Here are a few scientifically proven benefits to exercise, along with loving your reflection:

Increases stress resilience: Studies show exercise reorganizes the brain so that it is more resistant to stress. It does this by stopping the neurons firing in the regions of the brain thought to be important in the stress response (the ventral hippocampus).

Reduces anxiety: Studies have stated that exercise has a relatively long-lasting protective effect against anxiety. Both low and medium intensity exercise has been shown to reduce anxiety; those doing high intensity exercise are likely to experience the greatest reduction in anxiety, especially among women.

Lower dementia risk: Almost any type of exercise that gets your heart working reduces the risk of dementia. A review of 130 different studies found that exercise helped prevent dementia and mild cognitive impairment among participants. Regular exercise in midlife was associated with lower levels of cognitive problems. The participants who exercised also had better spatial memory.

Mood regulation: If you want to raise your energy levels, reduce tension, and boost mood, you can try talking to your friends or listening to music; however, most agree this is not always an easy job. Exercise allows you to regulate moods, especially not relying on an outside source.

Reduction in prescription medication: I am not a doctor, yet by all accounts a balanced body coincides with a balanced mind. A balanced mind creates synergy, allowing communication from the brain and nervous system to coincide with healthy organ function. In turn, you may be able to toss those high blood pressure meds out for good, amongst others.

Reduction in serious mental disorders: Schizophrenia is treated as a serious mental disorder. Stating hallucinations, paranoia, and confused thinking are deemed as schizophrenia. Despite the grave diagnosis of such a "disorder," there is evidence that exercise can help with all such symptoms, as well as alcoholism and body image issues.

Reduce silent strokes: A silent stroke is one that seems to have no outward symptoms, but can actually damage the brain. Without knowing why, sufferers can start experiencing more falls, memory problems, and difficulty moving. Exercise, though, reduces the chance of these symptoms and silent strokes by 40%.

Stimulate brain cell growth: Part of the reason that exercise is beneficial in so many different mental areas is that it helps new brain cells to grow. Again, studies show the brain regions related to memory and learning have increased cell growth and functioning. Allowing you to switch tasks efficiently, ignore distractions, and make plans and so on. This makes me wonder what is going on with each generation as we see so many people looking down at phones, constantly checking messages, not having conversation with others except through text messages. Not so stimulating.

Better sleep: The relationship between exercise and sleep is a little more complicated than most imagine. It's not necessarily the case that exercise makes you tired, so you sleep better. For example, a study on insomniacs found that 45 minutes on the treadmill did not make them sleep better that night. What has been proven were the long-term benefits which showed a 16-week program proved to allow insomniacs to receive better and more effective sleep patterns.

It's more fun than we predict: This is really what we're after. The final effect exercise has on the mind is not so ground-breaking, yet is the toughest to wrap our minds around. If you believe exercise is a 'chore,' let's reset that way of thinking. According to research, it's noted that beginning an exercise program can be a drag, at first. Once it becomes routine, a habit, most people enjoy their workouts much more than they predicted. Once main reason is to not put expectations on what you are unsure of. Have fun with it, and have fun with the benefits as well.

Now that we understand how exercise can benefit our mind, bodies, and soul, I not only practice what I preach, I teach others as well. Supplements are equally as important, yet are not so black and white. As you grow in your physically activity, it's important to align with an expert and discuss where you may need to add or delete certain vitamins, enzymes, and nutrients.

I use a product every single day which promotes healthy cell rebuilding as well as allowing my body to create its own antioxidants to naturally help my body to heal and repair. It utilizes five proprietary natural ingredients: *Milk Thistle Extract, Bacopa,*

Ashwaganda, Green Tea Extract and Turmeric Extract. I will even attest to while I was bit three times during relic hunts this year from tics, I had not realized I had contracted Lyme disease. I pushed through at the time, not knowing what I was truly up against, yet the will to continue to build my physically ability was also building my mental ability and helped to heal myself of the disease within six months. I am not suggesting you push through potentially harmful or life-threatening circumstances you may face; what I am saying is a strong mind, knowing what you are truly up against, and the ability to overcome through your will to achieve will serve you as you pull upon this intuitive nature, getting to know yourself and value that which you do reflect upon.

Now as I travel around the world, speaking, coaching, and helping others, I do so with confidence and compassion.

Listen to your body: There was a time I thought caffeine was so bad for you that I stopped drinking anything with caffeine in it. It's not the caffeine that is the problem—it's the additives like sugars and flour that become the true problem. If you are a runner, you should know that caffeine is not harmful; in fact, it is very helpful, naturally building energy and blood flow for a runner's body. It helps you adjust to climates and even altitude. I also utilize caffeine in a nutritional, hydrating coffee when I wasn't a coffee drinker before. I consulted a friend of mine, a worldwide champion marathon winner, about the use of caffeine as I know so many that have used performance-enhancing type products that I put caffeine in this category, a category of which it does not belong. Again, not all caffeinated products are created equal, so I sought out a nutritional coffee which not only helps the body hydrate as you drink water, especially for runners, it allows your body to retain nutrients and eliminate that which your body need not absorb. I recommend this to all of my clients as I have seen the ugly side here too, and there are always solutions, healthy solutions to increase your fitness level and allow focus and clarity. Do not settle for anything less than that which is truly beneficially natural to assist you in work, life, and physical balance.

There is no better way to lead than by example. I watched my son lose weight and QUIT smoking by the example of which I was setting. *If you're a parent, you know there is nothing more rewarding than to see your children make healthy life choices because of your actions.* Again, *lead by example and others will follow—actions speak louder than words.*

I am so humbled and grateful I took the time to research and learn through my own trials and failures to raise the level of my own pull towards health and fitness. When people I've worked with in the past come up and share their amazing stories of rebuilding their minds and life through my program, it is all the gratitude I can possibly ask for. There was a time I absolutely struggled with 'making myself get up and get going' and now that it is a habit, *it's a way of life.*

Walk with me on a visionary journey; *imagine waking up every day without having to talk yourself into getting up and going! Imagine a life where health and fitness are scheduled into your day. It doesn't haunt your mind as something you need to go and do—it is simply scheduled and accomplished. How does that feel?*

Notice how you may be feeling as you see yourself achieving the goals you've set to extend your life. Have your shoulders dropped a little? Are you breathing comfortably as you picture the ease of daily activities? Life is in balance, because you decided to decide.

Equally important is allowing yourself to give in to some fun with food too! If it's your birthday, by all means, have a piece of cake… you will realize moderation is the key and celebration unlocks any door towards all things which are possible.

Give yourself a break! Enjoy every step of your journey. Reflect upon that which serves you and that which does not and let go. You will begin to notice what works for you and what does not, by looking at your reflection and reflecting on the love and power that lies within you. Look in the mirror and look into your eyes. Stare at them and tell yourself you are bold, brilliant, and loved. Every day reflect upon your reflection!

To Contact Bill:

Email: billsdectors@verizon.net

Facebook: www.facebook.com/bill.leydic.9

YouTube: https://www.youtube.com/user/BillTheRelic

Twitter: @billleydic

Instagram billleydic

Phone: 412-600-8117

Charlene Renaud

Charlene Renaud is a proud member of the Canadian Association of Professional Speakers, Global Speakers Federation, and the Certified Coaches Federation. She has a wealth of knowledge, memorable stories, and life experience to share through her gifts of speaking and writing. She inspires people to heal, forgive, love, believe, transform, and lead! Charlene has been in policing for 22 years and has seen the heartache that people with mental illness and/or drug addiction endure, moving her towards leading and partaking in many drug education events, as well as helping people with addiction or trauma.

Charlene is a professional singer and has performed at numerous functions and community events, including singing national anthems for the Detroit Tigers. She has organized singing contests and fundraisers. Charlene wrote the Highway 401 song in honor of her fallen colleagues at the OPP and victims of Canada's worst highway disaster in 1999. The song created awareness about highway safety and raised money for the Children's Hospital of Toronto.

Charlene has spoken professionally at hundreds of events and is passionate about helping people in their life journey, having experienced major struggles, transformation, and extraordinary moments in her life.

Areas of expertise: Relationships, Self-Awareness, Addiction, Inspiration

The Piñata Theory

What's "Stuffed" Inside of YOU?

By Charlene Renaud

A Piñata is a colorful animal made of paper mache filled with candy and toys. Excited children line up at parties, anxiously waiting for their turn to be blindfolded and given a stick, to strike a Piñata, with the hopes of bursting it open. The lucky strike will spill the Piñata's contents onto the floor, causing the children to scatter like mice to hoard every piece. Where did a child's desire for candy come from? It is the result of the child's 'data bank' (i.e., subconscious mind) being downloaded with information from the 'downloader' (e.g., a teacher, parent, caregiver, relative, society) with the data that you can hit a paper animal, burst it open and be rewarded with candy. Thus, the child learns *candy is delicious; it is a prize or a reward.*

Let us now consider a metaphor. The inside of a Piñata is stuffed with goodies, and in order to get the gems, one must burst it open. Think of yourself as a Piñata and ask yourself, what's stuffed inside of me? From conception, you have been 'stuffed' or downloaded with masses of information, beliefs, pictures, experiences, and so on. All of your 'stuffing' is stored in your data bank. In order to crack your Piñata's code, you need to look at what you were stuffed with by examining what has been downloaded. Determine if it is good stuffing, bad stuffing, factual stuffing, silly stuffing, family dynamic stuffing, cultural stuffing, self-image stuffing, (un)healthy stuffing, religious stuffing … da fluff in da trunk! Remember, you had no control over most of what you downloaded. You were a Baby Piñata with no filter and you absorbed everything.

In my upcoming book *The Piñata Theory*, I will expand upon multiple types and sources of stuffing (e.g., education, religion, family, ancestry, bullying, abuse, global coordinates, racism, internet, media, addiction) to help you dissect and understand 'Your Personal Piñata.' You will flush out toxic, painful, or unhealthy stuffing, giving it the big boot it deserves! Your new Piñata will be able to guard itself against the little sticks trying to break it down while still holding on to the brilliant gems (i.e., candies) inside. I will walk you through the importance of downloading delicious new stuffing and rocking your Piñata's beautiful colors! And, please, don't get your stuffing in a knot when I refer to you as a Piñata. It is a metaphor and a fun visual tool meant to teach and inspire you and trigger your giggle button.

What's stuffed inside of you? Why does it matter? This is what I'd like to tickle you with in this chapter. Your past life experiences (e.g., your ethnicity, religious or spiritual beliefs, your address on the planet, your family life, your education, traumatic events, relationships) are stored like data inside your Piñata's subconscious mind. This stuffing or hidden data powerfully influences every moment of your life today. It can be damaging and paralyzing like kryptonite to Superman or transforming and life changing like an Olympic medal to an athlete. Your inside stuff affects your automatic responses, emotions, and decisions. What if you could consciously sift through the layers of stuffing in your Piñata's data bank and select what's in your best immediate and long-term interests? Do you have the conscious power and ability to do that? Do you have the ability to override or diminish the effects of destructive stuffing? Can you put more stuffing in your Piñata? Yes, yes, yes. Absolutely!

My Piñata idea came to me while speaking to Tracy of Lamourie Public Relations & Marketing in Toronto. I told Tracy that I had hit rock bottom in my life, resulting in me seeking the help of a phenomenal psychologist named Manny. He helped me dissect and "bust open my subconscious mind, like busting open a Piñata." I cured my addiction of fixing others by focusing on self-love.

Tracy loved the analogy about the Piñata and said that I was here to teach others. My life purpose is to teach others and my book *The Piñata Theory* is the metaphorical conduit. After that revealing conversation with Tracy, I began to write the book that my Aunt Helen had encouraged me to write for years. The knowledge and information I share in *The Piñata Theory* is derived from my personal experiences in examining how my stuffing affected my life. I have also worked for twenty-two years in policing and have witnessed vast differences in people's perceptions, beliefs, lifestyles, health, and expectations. In addition, as a singer, I have had the opportunity to meet hundreds of people. Why are people all different? Because, no two Piñatas are stuffed the same!

***

Hitting rock bottom refers to a mentally abusive relationship that began in late 2006. We married in 2009, despite pleas from my family and friends not to. I was a fixer type, who mistakenly thought I could blend into his severely dysfunctional family. I was under constant, deliberate abuse by his children with no substantive intervention by my husband. The stress led to painful fibromyalgia throughout my body. In 2012, my Piñata suffered a major mental psychosis. The relationship ended in divorce and rebuilding my life began. Coincidentally, my ex-husband's second wife developed serious mental health issues during their marriage before taking her own life. He told me she was crazy.

Dear Piñatas, when we blame people or circumstances for our troubles, we are not focusing our energy on where it needs to be—on us! When our Piñatas are picking dysfunctional lifestyles, not living our purpose, or not achieving our goals, we need to ask: what's inside of me that is holding me back? When we are strong internally—meaning a well-balanced Piñata—we make healthy, loving choices in our lives.

One time, Frank, a friend of my family, said, "You have a broken chooser."

I asked Frank to repeat that statement; puzzled by a phrase I'd never heard of. "A what?"

Frank repeated, "A broken chooser."

Then he added, "Your chooser is broken, but it's repairable."

My mate chooser was filled with unhealthy concepts about relationships and low self-esteem stuffing that I had gathered throughout childhood and adolescence. I was addicted to fixing others at the expense of my own wellness. Is your chooser broken? Do you need to repair a few bugs or do you need reprogramming? Remember, your chooser extracts data from your past. To be a healthy, happy Piñata, you need to digest new data that will help you, not keep you stuck.

THAT'S WHY YOU NEED TO EXAMINE YOUR STUFFING

In order to transform your life, you need to objectively look at your stuffing! I had a lot of unhealthy stuffing that I needed to examine and dissect in order to figure out some of my automatic, unconscious decisions. I compassionately began to see and understand (as you will) that I was extracting solely from my dated, pre-loaded stuffing. It took a lot of work to pick out that stuffing. It involved diving head first into my subconscious mind. Some of the stuffing in my Piñata was stored inside of me for a long time. Examining my old stuffing at times was painful. Some of the data or saved memories made me smile or laugh. Some made me visualize Dr. Phil asking me, "What were you thinking?" My subconscious mind drove the bus, and I sat in the backseat wondering when the bumpy ride was going to end. Are you feeling bumps in your life? Are you holding on to something that you won't let go? I'm going to explain how to put your Piñata back into the driver's seat!

FIRST, YOU NEED TO UNDERSTAND THE CONSCIOUS AND SUBCONSCIOUS MIND

Your Piñata has two minds: the conscious (aware) and subconscious (hidden) mind.

The conscious mind is your awareness, the part of your mind that makes intentional choices. For example, when you get up in the morning, your conscious mind decides what to wear. When your Piñata sleeps, so does your conscious mind. You are out for the count! Well, at least this half of your brain!

On the other hand, the subconscious mind runs 24/7, in the background, and functions without your awareness. It's a data bank filled with every life experience that you have ever had and everything you have learned: your stuffing. The subconscious mind does not discern what is true or false. Its job is to store data to extract later. It is your hard drive, containing your life data. Your subconscious mind allows you to drive your car every day automatically as a pre-learned experience. The data in your subconscious mind can also activate automatic feelings, responses, or emotions based on the stuffing downloaded into it.

Example: Peter Piñata is driving along feeling happy until a song comes on the radio. This song was the song he danced to with his bride at their wedding. The marriage ended, causing Peter Piñata to become angry, hurt, and depressed. When Peter Piñata listens to this song now, his subconscious mind automatically triggers hurtful feelings, based on his experience. This song, even though the marriage may have ended years ago, produces pain. The subconscious mind is powerful, until you discover how it works, how to control it, and how to reprogram it!

The good news is that we Piñatas are intelligent and resilient. We can train our conscious mind to recognize when our subconscious mind is fueling responses, feelings, or emotions. It's like our Piñata has two brains. One is a data bank, the subconscious filled with all sorts of stuffing, and one is a choice maker, the conscious mind. Your chooser automatically and unconsciously extracts information from your data bank, which is loaded with helpful, healthy information or faulty, damaging information. The conscious side of your Piñata's brain must interject and control things in the moment instead of allowing the subconscious mind to run wild—responding solely on past experience, behavior, or knowledge.

Let's refer to Peter Piñata's reaction to his wedding song as an example of how the conscious mind can override the subconscious mind. When he starts to feel pain, he will apply the Piñata Mind-Shift! He says with confidence, "Hold that response! Today I know that I cannot change what has happened in the past. I know today that I consciously choose a new response to this song. I accept it as is. I am better off in my life today, being free of a relationship that no longer involved truth or love. I am happy today and on track to fulfilling my destiny."

I'd like you to think about your triggers or disappointments and before you respond, honestly evaluate and accept <u>what has happened in the past is unchangeable</u>. Think about all of the things that you could do today without limitations or chains from the past. Peter Piñata successfully stopped a painful response and kicked that stuffing to the curb. Remember, you are in the driver's seat and can consciously override and rewrite new experiences. Apply the Piñata Mind-Shift in any situation where you feel you are hurting yourself or others; where you want to accept, forgive, grow, and be a Leader Piñata. Any type of feeling, thought, or trigger (e.g., song, person, place) that hurts you in some way will remain status quo until you stop and consciously override previous automatic responses.

To heal your Piñata, you must go back to the place or time of the pain and heal it now. Many people hold on to stinky stuffing for years and don't realize the impact it has on their everyday life. It builds resentment, diminishes potential, creates division, causes pain, breeds disease, and steals their joy. Direct your needs or desires to God (or a Higher Power or Creator or a Universal Source) asking for guidance in the things you struggle with.

Charlene's Little Red Wagon Piñata Challenge

Think about a person who has hurt you and visualize that you are pulling them in a little red wagon all day long. Try not to push them over a cliff, ok? You bring them everywhere: to work, to church, to the grocery store, to the bathroom (Oh no!), and finally to the foot of your bed. Your Piñata sleeps waiting for a fresh start tomorrow. The next morning, you wake up and as soon as your feet hit the floor, you grab the handle on the wagon and start pulling the person around with you all day. Again! This is what essentially happens when you do not let go of the past: you suffer strain, pulling the weight of someone or something around with you *today*. Your arm, your heart, and your mind will endure unnecessary stress. How much can you take, my dear Piñata? Will you reach the breaking point? Why endure, suffer, strain, or break when you instead can be joyful, healthy, accepting, and forgiving?

Is changing old ways easy? No, it isn't. <u>Change is a choice</u>. Repetitious choices become patterns or behaviors. When you move into a life that focuses on wellness, forgiveness, truth, and love, life becomes clearer. Consciously loading fresh, positive stuffing into your Piñata will create a new reality; stuffing from the past will become inconsequential. When you examine your past, you may remember moments that you weren't proud of. Human Piñatas make mistakes. Being the product of our minds, we worked with the data we had at the time and didn't know better (or knew better and did it anyway). With our new knowledge, we grow and learn—forgiving ourselves and others.

BECOMING A LEADER PIÑATA

Leader Piñatas have a purpose: a knowing and a desire to share their gifts and talents with the world to make it a better place. Leader Piñatas are mindful of what they digest into their body, mind, and spirit. They have a high level of intelligence and know there is more beyond what we see, hear, smell, and touch. A key trait of a Leader Piñata is they listen to their inner voice. Their knowledge and direction comes from a non-human source: God. They create music, art, and new inventions; humbly revealing that these gifts came from a higher power and they were simply the instrument. These leaders have an inner spirit that is on fire. They strive to live the way the higher power directs them.

THE SPIRIT INSIDE YOUR PIÑATA

Although we live in a human world, you and I are gifted with a spirit, which is separate from the conscious and subconscious mind. The spirit exists within your Piñata's shell and is the opposite of human-made stuffing that can be ego-based, fearful, painful, flawed, and limited. Your spirit is connected to a divine source that is truth, love, and unlimited potential. The spirit is a natural knowing that speaks to us. In order to live a spirit-filled existence, one must acknowledge the spirit within and trust in God to provide us with flawless, life-changing truth. Many times, I have prayed and asked God to guide me, where I knew I was flawed and needed change. I had to release old thoughts, actions, and ways to be led by the Holy Spirit.

Sparkling Piñata Tip: When you begin changing damaging ways, God will open doors for you, synchronicity happens, and the right people will appear in your life.

Our spirit is the seed of truth and wisdom, planted within us and within every cell of life, from a source that is powerful beyond measure. Our spirit is a gift from God! It is 'God's Amazing Stuffing,' a part of Him in us, our means of connectedness with Him, to be further expanded upon in my book *The Piñata Theory*.

God is the master planner, the all-mighty and the all-knowing. God is the source of love, forgiveness, and miracles. God made all that is in the universe. He has a divine plan for your life. Once you draw upon all that ever was and ever will be, the richer your life will be. You become a beacon of light, leading others to a new way of living. Our spirit is also aware that there is something more, beyond things, money, titles, and ego. It can see and feel deeply the frailty of humanity and the planet. We are experiencing the effects of terrorism, war, and global warming to the point of the pending collapse of mankind, the animal kingdom, and Mother Earth. Perhaps this is why you are reading this book. Are you a Leader Piñata? An agent of change, leading humanity towards peace, love, equality, and abundance for all? What can you do to change the world? What gifts do you have to share that will heal, save, change, bring joy, or inspire? Some Piñatas are fortunate to be, or have, amazing mentors in their life. Mentor Piñatas share their beautiful stuffing; they believe in us, encourage us, and help us see and reach our highest potential.

Sparkling Piñata Tip: Take another Piñata under your wing and witness the fruit of knowledge, love, and connection.

***

Decades ago, I was a shy girl from a farm. I can remember lying on a hill with my cousin Rachelle looking up at the beautiful blue sky and floating fluffy clouds. We voiced our dreams and sent them into the universe. We would stand on a wagon as our stage and use a cob of corn as our microphone. I would visualize singing and speaking to crowds of people. I knew I wanted to make people happy and change the world. Little did I know that God was watching. As a professional speaker and author, I guide people in areas of wellness, addiction, relationships, and overcoming trauma.

***

Charlene Renaud

(Ontario, Canada)

www.charlenerenaud.com

info@charlenerenaud.com

Tel: 519-436-3911

David Ribott-Bracero

David Ribott-Bracero, EdD (ABD), is a leadership coach whose mission it is to disrupt the "business as usual" mindset to move clients from comfort zone to growth zone in service of their leadership and learning. Originally a sports coach, who later certified as a life coach and business coach, David has been working in Leadership & Learning & Development for over 17 years and remains driven to create the conditions for sustainable success for people and organizations. His commitment for sustainable success is grounded in his belief that all people, and organizations, can enhance and align their performances when the right conditions for success are cultivated with deliberate intention.

David's journey began in New York City as an educator before transitioning to Seoul, Korea, where he split his time between the worlds of higher education and HR L&D. He currently serves on the Board of Directors for the International Coach Federation in the UAE, mentors coaches in certification training, and provides expertise as a Senior Leadership & Learning Business Partner to Abu Dhabi Police PSG. In early 2017, the World Coaching Congress will honor David with the **100 Best Global Coaching Leaders Award**.

A Fight to Change

By David Ribott-Bracero

Growing up in the Bronx, NYC, you get a sense of who you are early in life because you're constantly tested with challenges, temptations, and the unforeseen nature that is ever-evolving change. Add into the mix the starting point of abject poverty, and you have yourself the perfect blend of broken dreams and unrealized promise. I knew then the promise of a normal life was not going to come easy for me. And what is a normal life anyway?!? At the time, I didn't know it, but what I was going to have to embark on was to change my circumstances if I was going to have a chance at living. Let me be clear, being alive doesn't constitute living, for surviving does not create any measure of a good quality of life.

Most people I call family and friend understood how to survive—you fight! Needless to say, the fighting spirit was nurtured and cultivated in me. I fed it on a daily basis…….it was a driver for me to stay motivated when the outlook was beyond bleak……it was my principal strategy to reframe any situation……got no money to take the train to wherever I needed to go, no problem—I'll walk there. It didn't matter that the walk added an hour or so to my trip. The "fight" in me was enough to fuel me with a razor sharp focus that made the experience cathartic. It served as a personal reminder of the environment I was a part of, and equally wanted no part of for my future.

One thing about living with the "fight" in you, the fight in us rewires the way we think and our behavior towards the world, and I was no different. The anger I lived with gave me an edge. Some non-New Yorkers call it standoffish, but native New Yorkers call it attitude and I convinced myself it was ok because I was doing what was necessary to make it out of my environment and change my situation.

Recognizing the breadth and depth of your environment is key to unlocking a path to the realization of your potential. My environment of growing up in the South Bronx in the late 80's and early 90's wasn't ideal, but the "fight" in me was my equalizer in times when a lack of access to resources was a barrier to success. Dare I say, it bred a specific kind of New York attitude, a *f*#k you* attitude, which only deepened my resolve to fight on. Though at the time, conversely, I did have the clarity to notice fighting for the sake of fighting or applying a *f*ck you* attitude was a reactive response to my environment and the situations it threw at me—great for fueling anger for the "fight," but not representative of a greater command of my drive to convert dire circumstances into success.

Luckily for me, I had the outlet of playing sports. In particular, I had the controlled-anger-friendly domain that is football to cultivate my craft. Here I was able to put into practice my ability to leverage the "fight" in me to fuel anger that I further converted into a high level of performance on the field—the ultimate outcome and one I needed to experience. I needed the reinforcement of knowing I could impact outcomes in the way I desired to. I was on the right path I thought (or at least, the right path for that time in my life). Playing with controlled anger made me a good player, it helped me get named Team Captain, and the teams I led won multiple championship titles, but that was on the field. And while there was some transferability of football to the streets of the South Bronx, Marshall Goldsmith got it right when he wrote, "what got you here, won't get you there," and my "there" was understanding what I wanted to get out of life— my bigger picture.

An Impactful Conversation

The pivotal trigger for me was a conversation I had with my football coach before graduating from high school where he asked, *"what do you want to do with your life?"* In my mind, I thought it was serendipitous because I was asking myself that same question, but the timing of it felt like a trick question and like he was setting me up for some comedic hook where I'd be the joke at the end of it. But that wasn't the case. He was serious and the conversation changed the way I looked at personal behavior and achievement:

Coach: What do I want to do when you get older?

Me: I want to work.

Coach: So, what do you want to do?

Me: I want to get a job and support myself….be independent.

Coach: Ok, what does that look like?

Me: I don't know.

Coach: What do you need to do to make it happen?

Me: ….I don't know.

Unconsciously, and I wouldn't realize it for years, but a deeper appreciation for the relationship between design and performance began making sense to me that day. By design and performance, I mean how the make-up of something impacts an outcome. Take the design of a sports car, for example, and how it correlates to topflight racing—the outcome. One is enabled to some extent because of the other. While this is a simplified version of the concept, simple was what I needed then because it gave me just enough clarity to make better decisions about my immediate future, my undergrad college years, and my early career development.

The Changing of My Environment

On September 19, 2001, I finally changed my environment and left the Bronx, NYC, for Seoul, South Korea. While I was excited to be there, my first night in I couldn't sleep. Confident when I first boarded my flight from JFK airport to Incheon airport to my new home, in Korea, I felt bewildered at a foreign feeling I just couldn't shake…the feeling was vulnerability. Vulnerability—what's that? The anger, which fueled the command and control of my "fight," worked like a repellent against vulnerability in the past. Uncomfortable as it was this time around, I was equally intrigued by the challenge of overcoming it. Remember, the "fight" needs an obstacle to overcome, an enemy to defeat, a puzzle to solve to define accomplishment and success, so I plowed on.

Those first few years in Seoul never saw me get past Kubler-Ross' Stages of Change cycle of shock-denial-frustration and because from an early age I had a chip on my shoulder, I was comfortable bringing the "fight" with me from my old environment to my new one. Flawed as that may sound now, it felt like a winning strategy. My professional success only helped to encourage further reasoning that way of thinking was working. And why not—wherever I worked, I was the youngest among my peers. Where tradition says you develop one career, I developed two paths simultaneously: one as university faculty and the other in HR Learning & Development. But inside, I still couldn't shake this nagging feeling. Vulnerability. This time around, this feeling was determined to teach me something, and it wasn't going away on its own.

Saying Goodbye to the "Fight"

Experiencing calm is a strange occurrence to a lifelong fighter. Calm naturally softens the fire, readiness, and willingness to fight. That was a scary place to be for me when all I'd ever known was to access the strength to fight, the courage to fight, and the willingness to fight. But here I didn't feel compelled to access the "fight" anymore. By design, I created the "fight" and it led me to achieve whatever I set out to do despite the challenges of my old environment, but the urge to lean into it wasn't strong anymore.

In letting the "fight" slowly dissipate, I began to access courage in a different way. I channeled it to help me to look even deeper at myself. My environment in Korea, for all the challenges it presented, was not the problem. Frankly speaking, I wasn't born to Korean parents. I was born to Puerto Rican parents. I didn't grow up in Seoul. No, it was my choice to take a job there. It was all my doing—I ended up there because of a decision I made, so no one was to blame, and there was no reason to be angry.

And I wasn't angry anymore, but I was scared because I began noticing what was waiting for me would be difficult. Deep in my heart, I knew this wasn't going to be easy since it meant looking at myself at a way I hadn't before, for who I was, and wasn't, without the "fight" guiding me. The "fight" had been my friend when I needed someone I could trust to have my back. But I was holding on to it though it no longer served me, the evolving me in my new environment.

I recall a Buddhist story a friend shared that unlocked this deeper understanding of holding on and letting go. The story goes, and I'll paraphrase of course,

> *A young boy was stranded on a piece of land wanting to cross a body of water to the other side to continue his journey. The body of water was too vast and his ability to swim not strong enough for him to swim across. Nearing despair, an empty boat came into his view and he used it to paddle to the other side. Once there, he was grateful to the boat for appearing, for helping him on his journey, for saving his life. But he was conflicted with what to do with the boat—should he bring it with him? He felt indebted, for had the boat not appeared, he might well have starved to death while trying to figure out how to get across the water. He eventually left the boat to continue his journey.*

In this story, I understood the "fight" was my boat and getting across the water to continue the journey was akin to the need to adapt to my new environment, and let go of the past.

My self-image then wouldn't let me admit it openly because it was foreign to me, but I was in meditation. I now know the practice is called productive meditation, and it would serve to provoke a deep internal cleanse. In short, it would help me see what I couldn't see, what the "fight" had protected me from—I had moved past the Stages of Change cycle of shock-denial-frustration, but was stuck at Depression. This realization was tough because, again, my self-image associated depression with weakness. A true awakening occurred when things bottomed out for me on the way to work one morning. That day I found myself trying to access the anger of the "fight" to deal with a personal matter that remained unresolved. Like that moment in a suspense movie when the antagonist is revealed, the other shoe had dropped for me, and I was the antagonist to my own protagonist.

I'm a student and historian of the game of boxing. Growing up in New York, boxing held a deep and special connection. It was the birthplace of Everlast, Gleason's Gym, home to Sugar Ray Robinson, Iron Mike Tyson, and the famed Madison Square Garden, and being Puerto Rican to boot, to love boxing was a birth rite. There are moments when boxers are in training, where they shadow box, often times in front of a mirror. In these moments, they come face-to-face with their reflection. Being able to see yourself in the mirror, to not look away, to hold yourself accountable, to say yes I am who I see in my reflection, is an empowering feeling. When your reflection is not who you see yourself to be, then you have arrived at your moment of truth. How you respond will dictate where you go from there. Not ready to see yourself, and you only prolong the agony and possibly spiral out of control. Ready to see yourself, and begin confronting some hard truths.

When I looked at the mirror to see "my reflection," I saw someone lost, but not angry, someone confused, but possessing self-compassion, someone in search of something, and practicing patience—who was this person I thought? I had changed with my new environment. Gone was the need to call on the "fight" to get me through. In its place was patience and self-compassion. Attributes always a part of me, but never the driver for getting things done.

I felt peace and the pull of new possibilities that could be achieved without the "fight," so I said goodbye to my friend and left Seoul with the lessons in personal change I needed for future challenges that lay in wait.

The Day of My Tsunami - Life Forever Changed

I didn't know it the morning of July 12, 2008, but that summer afternoon on a scorching hot Abu Dhabi road, my life forever changed. On that day, I was injured in a terrible car accident. Like in an earthquake that has subsided, you survey your surroundings to see what has been destroyed, what can be salvaged, and what needs to be built from scratch. (I'll spare you the gruesome details only to share I needed reconstructive hand surgery, nine operations in all, over a period of nearly five years, all on my left hand—my dominant hand.)

Once I got past the "I'm grateful to be alive" phase, I was quickly taken by a sunken feeling things would never be the same again. Before that day, I was invincible because I proved I could make it in the challenging jungle that is the Bronx and look deep into myself to adjust my approach to the ways of a new environment in Seoul, but never was my self-image shattered—now it was.

Previously, I let my anger fuel my determination to succeed. But I was no longer angry…….I was wounded, no longer in control. It wasn't about succeeding anymore, it was about learning how to live with permanent disfigurement to my hand…..and the car accident was another "reflection in the mirror" moment where I realized I never really learned how to live without a certain self-image. I knew how to survive, how to fight, how to win, and even how to adjust, but to live with cracks to my self-image, to see myself as permanently limited in what I could do with my hand, to be partially disabled, shook me to the core.

So much of my development had taken shape by defining myself against my environments, whether in the Bronx or Seoul—my outer world. But my inner world—the part of me comprised of my beliefs, ethics, values, and greater mission and vision for my place in the world to be my guide to "live"—wasn't given the same amount of attention, nor the same amount of effort, and it finally caught up with me.

Time for a Systems Upgrade

Years after, when I was completely healed, and fully understood what it meant to "live," I understood I had experienced a transformation in those years in recovery from the car accident. Then, I didn't have the language nor wisdom to articulate what I had undergone, but years later when I entered the world of professional coaching, I experienced a moment of clarity while training—I upgraded my internal operating system.

When I say operating system—I mean our internal structure, the design that creates the capacity for us to perform. In today's world of personal computers, those who use Apple probably have OS X El Capitan, while Window's users have Windows 10. To use a metaphor, the operating system I put to use from 2008 to 2012 was Windows 97 and long past its date of optimal use. Where once my ambition had burned the fire of the "fight" to get things done, my ego had slowly taken hold to corrupt my system and blinded me to it in the process. The takeover from the voice of my ambition to the voice of my ego was subtle, but it's wasn't until I noticed the voice holding me back from my recovery that I realized, *"this isn't working anymore."*

An Ending with More Learning and New Beginnings

The gift of realizing I was living with ego as my driver was to see I was creating unnecessary challenges. Though it had helped me "win" along the way, the wins were at the expense of my ability to thrive in the way one is able to move beyond survival to truly "live."

What this transformational change afforded me was the opportunity to bring clarity, wisdom, and purpose into my life—to live without ego by design.

I often get asked do I regret getting injured in my car accident. Every time I'm asked, I share the Chinese Proverb, "what is good can become bad, and what is bad can become good." It reminds me to always have perspective and to see the "cost and benefit" to any and everything. Yes, my dominant hand is now slightly deformed, but it didn't prevent me from learning how to play tennis and squash with my other hand. And for a brief time, I was even writing with my right hand. But, ultimately the benefit of the car accident was coming to see my ego and I needed to part ways.

It was by no means a simple process, but once the ego was less dominant, I was ready to confront insecurities holding me back in my evolution as a man with clarity, wisdom, and purpose. The culmination of this came on May 13, 2015, when Leo Matias gave me the gift of becoming his father.

So, as we come to a close, I ask you to take a moment and ask yourself, *"what must end for something new to begin in order for me to experience the gifts of truly living?"*

***

To Contact David:

david@leadershipcoach.me.

https://ae.linkedin.com/in/davidribott

Dawn Lee

Dawn Lee is a Professional Coach, Spiritual Development Mentor, and catalyst for positive lasting change. She is the founder of The Cognitive Soul, an Intuitive Coaching Practice and movement for those ready to hear, ready to heal, and ready to massively change their lives. Originally from Scotland, Dawn now lives in Brisbane, Australia.

Her mission is to help rid the world of the endemic *not good enough* belief that dims light and stops people from truly living. And to remind others of their energetic and spiritual nature and that they matter. Her gift is helping others heal their hearts and transform past pain and trauma to experience amazing lives, regardless of what they've lived through.

She has a BA (Hons) Degree in Psychology and Sociology, is NLP trained, and is a Certified Energy and Chakra Body Clearing Practitioner. Dawn is a divine truth seeker, journeyer, thriver, and warrior for peace, love, and happiness. She's also a devoted mother to her beloved son and soul mate and a passionate advocate for health, healing, and the infinite power within.

Transforming Pain to Purpose—The Road Less Travelled to Peace, Love, & Happiness

By Dawn Lee

Love, connection, peace, joy, and prosperity flowing into your life. Take a deep breath, everything you want is waiting for you.

What if regardless of what you suffered or survived you could be happy and in love with your life?

What if you could find purpose in past pain or trauma? And that purpose was the key to unlocking your emotional freedom. Could a painful past actually work *for* you instead of *against* you?

Without dragging around the weight of your past, who could you be?

How much more fulfilling would your relationships be? Imagine what you could achieve if you finally stopped holding yourself back.

You; free from the past. Free from life's limiting beliefs and *not good enough* stories. Free from the need for approval or validation. Wildly alive, exactly where you're meant to be creating a reality you can thrive in.

A reality where confusion gently lifts like early morning fog. Leaving crystal-clear clarity that rebirths a brand new you. Like a butterfly, radically transformed as it emerges from its chrysalis.

Daily struggles give way to ease and flow. And everything begins to miraculously fall into place. As though the Universe were turning it on, just for you.

Of course there will still be storms, but your roots are strong. You're operating from the authentic part of who you are; wise, loving, and free. Wired into your own divine guidance and the infinite source within.

Sounds pretty amazing, right?

But perhaps you're wondering, "Is it *really* possible for me? Can I really be happy after everything I've been through?"

There's no wound too deep that can't be healed. No trauma too great that can't be transformed. I've helped transform countless painful stories. Stories of cancer, devastating marriage breakups, death of a child. Permanent paralysis, suicide of a loved one, fractured parental relationships, and deep, dark wounds from empty childhoods. Along with my own transformation, testimony to the human spirit's capacity to heal and transform.

To transform our story, we must be willing to give our belief system the mother of all shakes. We have to radically shift our perspective and unlearn what we know.

There are two fundamental elements to transforming a painful story into a heroic new narrative:

1. Knowing the energetic nature of ourselves and the Universe.

2. Connecting back to the truth of who were are and why we're here.

Even back then, I sensed there was a purpose for the darkness in my life. Of course I couldn't have told you what it was; the mind of a child knows of no such thing.

And yet the heart and soul have a wisdom beyond age and imagination. An infinite, guiding intelligence that softly whispers in stillness.

It's afternoon. A hazy, single sunbeam tenderly pours through an awkward gap between faded curtains. I'm 3 years old. I stand terrified in the centre of the living room. My mother is frantic. She's trying to flee the iron clutches of a drunk, enraged, irrational husband.

She lunges for the door. He beats her to it, violently slamming it shut with an almighty bang.

We're trapped.

Like a tiny statue I stand frozen, silent and helpless. A little girl enveloped by darkness, but for the gentle sunbeam caressing her face.

I watch as he pins her to the wall, vicious hands around her fragile throat. She's choking, crying, pleading to be let go as he taunts her through gritted teeth. His eyes red and ablaze with an uncontrollable rage.

I'll come to know this fear many times; my world is about to get darker.

There may be dark shadows in your world right now. I get it. I too have known the many shades of inky black. The dirty truth about life is it's a beautiful wilderness; it's also a painful one.

Everybody has stories of past hurt. Stories of family drama, messy breakups, and broken hearts. Stories of rejection, betrayal, deceit, and being treated as though they were disposable.

Loved ones we couldn't save. Bodies ravished by chronic disease and injury. Lost jobs, financial burden, and disasters that strike in the still of the night.

Violence, prejudice, abuse, rape, deprivation, injustice, and war penetrate the fragile fabric of humanity.

Search the planet over, you won't find a single human being untouched by trauma or tragedy. Everyone's been a victim of something or someone. Some ache many times.

The victim archetype is deeply ingrained in our psyche. Trapped in a culture of victimhood, we're obsessed by the past, afraid of the future. Locked into our wounds sometimes for decades.

Stress, anxiety, and depression have peaked new heights. Even in our young. Internal disconnect is endemic.

But we're entering an age of awakened consciousness. We're being called to awaken to the true nature of life and bring peace, love, and harmony into our world. But first we must bring it into ourselves.

According to Buddha, "Pain is inevitable, suffering is optional."

Pain is simply a feeling, an intense energy felt within the body. If we could learn to sit with pain until it passed, we'd release it. But instead we avoid our feelings and suppress our emotion. Stuffing it down with a cocktail of chemicals and unhealthy distractions, we then project it onto others.

It's not pain that's our problem—it's our resistance to it and as a result our lack of healing.

What inflicts suffering is the meaning we ascribe to painful events. It's the stories of unworthiness we create around our pain. And the torturous belief "*It shouldn't happen.*"

She shouldn't have hurt me. He shouldn't have died. They shouldn't have done it.

And yet they did. That's what's real. And as Byron Katie reminds us, when we argue with reality, we lose, but only 100% of the time.

It shouldn't have happened is a painful fantasy. An illusion that drives our suffering. If it happened, it was meant to. How could it be anything other than what it is? To change the outcome would be to change everything that led to it. It's impossible.

Surrendering to it having happened is not liking nor condoning it. It's simply accepting *what is so* we can allow our pain and begin the healing process from a place of truth.

So if we can't avoid pain, could we learn to drop our resistance to it? If we could learn to live in such a way as if we'd chosen every experience, would we still suffer?

The sexual abuse begins when I'm 5 and continues for another 6 years.

There are too many times to keep count. There's no pattern. No clear way to develop a strategy to protect myself, although I try.

I avoid his gaze at all times. I move through the house with the stealth of a soldier in enemy territory. I know he can appear at any time.

But it's the night that brings the greatest terror. I'm at my most vulnerable and he takes advantage.

So if pain had a purpose what could it be? If it exists *for* us, what does it want us to know?

Pain is a great teacher. It gives us depth and compassion. It also serves the soul's insatiable desire to expand consciousness.

"If you want to find the secrets of the Universe, think in terms of energy, frequency, and vibration." - Nikola Telsa

Feelings are energy. And like thoughts, beliefs, and words, they vibrate at specific frequencies. These vibrations influence the cells in our bodies. And like stones tossed into still water, ripple through us reaching out to others and beyond.

Energy attracts its like. What we're consistently vibrating at attracts itself back into our experience. If we hold on to our pain, we're sure to attract more of it.

Our feelings are also a sophisticated inbuilt guidance system, like a GPS. They alert us as to when we're in or out of alignment with the vibrational frequency of truth.

How many times have you felt in your gut that something wasn't quite right?

Feelings alert us to the vibrations of what we're thinking. The lower the frequency, the denser the energy. Low vibrating frequencies of shame and guilt, for example, feel heavy in our bodies.

A recent study in embodied cognition found guilt-induced memories led to increased reports of weight (Day and Bobocel 2013).

High vibrations of love, joy, and forgiveness on the other hand, evoke lightness. When we're in alignment with our best and highest good we feel alive, inspired, and on track.

You've experienced that, right?

Moving up the scale from lower to higher frequencies of joy is what we seek. Why else do you want that job, that house, that relationship, that car, that body, that holiday?

You want to be happy.

What we focus on influences not only our physiology, but our experience. We attract what we consistently think about. If we're reliving our trauma over and over again, we're creating our future through our past.

From early childhood, we're taught that negative emotions are bad. Children, being highly intuitive, have an inherent knowing when to release emotion. But we demonize their outbursts as temper tantrums, character flaws.

Our response is often punitive. Sent to the corner for time outs. Physical chastisement, the withdrawing of a favourite activity, or worse, our love. Quashing children's instinctive nature and natural responses shames and confuses their developing psyche.

In every moment, we're our children's teachers. And in the early years seed planters, programmers of the great subconscious mind. A negative reaction to emotion sends a clear message:

It's not ok to express yourself.

When you're emotional, I'm not here for you.

I raise my voice in anger to you.

I lower my vibration and withdraw my love from you.

And a belief is formed: *If I'm emotional, I'm not lovable. I cannot show up as true myself.*

Children repetitively exposed to negative energies and unloving behaviours such as criticism, neglect, shaming, over-controlling, perfectionism, and physical punishment typically develop a belief of unworthiness.

But a child's first experience of emotional pain (the *core wound*) is most significant. Typically, children experience a core wound around age 3 - 5. Egocentric and unable to rationalise thought, they blame themselves.

For example, divorce can create a core wound of abandonment. A parent's departure can be internalized as the child's fault. Dad left. He doesn't love me. I must be bad. No one will love me. Everyone will leave me.

Suppressing emotion around the event, the child familiarizes with being abandoned and forms a subconscious attachment to it. Along with a subconscious program for love; love hurts, love leaves.

Abandonment attracts more abandonment. Over time, the subconscious seeks out similar conditions to repeat the pattern. Hello cycle of dysfunctional relationships.

Like an invisible thread, core wound energy weaves it way through a person's life. Deepening and repeating until it's healed. It lies at the root of persistent relationship drama. Instigates chronic dis-ease and hides beneath excessive weight and the daily angst in our stomach.

Driving our recurring resentment and mistrust, it fuels our lack of self-belief and self-love. It demands our attention, always inviting us to turn inwards and unravel the many layers that block our inner light.

Could this be the purpose of the core wound? Could our wounds hold the seed of a divine plan to guide us back to our own spirituality? Is this what Rumi meant when he said *the wound is where the light enters?*

I'm 8 years old. I awaken in the night to whimpering sobs. I try not to listen, but it floods my brain. Pressure builds inside me and I burst.

"Go away!" I shout. "Leave us alone."

Silence. And then the door opens.

My mother steps into the room, a silhouette against the hallway light. "What's going on?" she asks.

My breath all but passes out of me. My heart is beating wildly against my small chest. Like moth wings on a hot light.

He responds she's hurt and he's comforting her. But he's never been a safe place to fall and she knows it.

Silently I scream inside; "Say something, do something!" But she turns, walks through the door, closing it softly behind her.

She takes with her hope and leaves behind a brutal realization. We won't be saved; not tonight.

Devastated, I pull the covers over my head, sinking into the little protection they offer me. My only hope now is self-preservation.

I hear him move. I sense him standing over me. I close my eyes tight before the weight of his closed fist hits. One single punch. Then he's gone.

As I lay in the darkness, I feel a heat arise within me. Like a fire lighting deep within my belly. And a soft voice silently whispers:

"Be strong. You will not be destroyed by him. There is something greater."

The next day, I awaken with a clear promise to myself. When I grow up, I will know happiness.

It would be years before I'd truly understand the message from my soul that dark night. I'd also come to know that before I was born, my soul planned my life; I chose my parents.

"This is the miracle: behind every condition, person, or situation that appears "bad" or "evil" lies concealed a deeper good. That deeper good reveals itself to you—both within and without—through inner acceptance of what is." - Eckhart Tolle

I know pain and trauma aren't welcome, especially to the innocent. I too wish we lived in a world of absolute peace, love, and harmony. I wish it for you and I wish it for me.

But that's not what's real. That's not our world, until it is.

Our world is one of duality. Everything has an opposite and neither can exist nor be known in the absence of the other. Without the darkness, we can't know the light. Without pain, we can't know pleasure. Without guilt; innocence. Hate; love. Sadness; joy etc.

Duality is the premise for all transformation.

What you want is the opposite of what you don't want. And wherever you are is the starting point for where you're going. In between is simply a matter of degrees.

Stop for a moment and imagine that the greater part of who you are is soul. Yes, we're human, but we're more. We're the furthest projection of source energy. Individuals, vibrating as a whole. We're one.

That you're a spiritual being having a human experience may be a familiar concept to you. But just how cleansed would your perspective be if you actually *owned* the notion?

If you could view life first as a soul and then as a human being, how different would life look?

Would you still perceive your experiences in the same way? Would you still believe in your own unworthiness? Knowing you're eternal, would you still fear death?

Soul comes from oneness. Oneness has no contrast. Duality provides the contrast required for transformation to occur. Perhaps we come to earth to experience contrast so that we can spiritually evolve.

According to James Hillman's *The Soul's Code,* as we grow up into life, the soul grows down into humanity. Pain and suffering carve out the necessary space for the soul to settle deeper into the human experience.

Could our painful experiences then be planned by the soul before birth? Do our wounds enable the fulfilment of a cosmic assignment to transform energies and raise the vibration of humanity?

Is it possible that what hurts us most, actually serves us most?

You may have already begun to notice that we're being pulled to raise our vibration and the vibration of our planet. But if we stay stuck mentally rehashing old victim stories and hating those who hurt us, we stay tuned to the frequency of our wounds and our hatred. These are the vibrations we offer up to the Universe.

Something miraculous happens when we consciously awaken. We become peaceful. Loving. Forgiving. We become of service to others, helping raise them up to their highest good.

The most inspiring teachers travel through the greatest adversity.

The late Wayne Dyer, abandoned by his alcoholic father, in and out of orphanages. Tony Robbins, beaten by his alcoholic, drug-addicted mother. Of whom he recently said, "If my mother had been the mother I'd wanted, I wouldn't be the man I am today."

Oprah, one of the most illuminous souls on the planet. Repeatedly molested by several family members. Secretly birthing a baby at the tender age of 14. Yet, like Tony Robbins, an influential powerhouse. Injecting love, hope, and inspiration into the hearts and minds of millions.

There are many defining moments in my own healing journey. Since leaving home at just 16, adventure, travel, laughter, education, love, and connection have become my lifelong medicine.

I've dug deep into my own shadow. First acknowledging and then transforming everything within me that didn't belong. Gratitude, forgiveness, love, trust, and a deep sense of value keep me connected to my spiritual nature.

Clear now of my purpose and place in this life, I adore who I am, who I'm becoming. And I live in awe of the child in me who courageously bore the brunt of my pain and suffering so that I could now carry this story heroically.

I tingle in knowing the truth of who I am and why I'm here. It drives my life, my business, my success, and my passion to love and serve.

Because of my past, I have an immense empathy and understanding for others' pain. And my story is now a guiding light for transformation.

Every painful experience offers us a choice. We can define ourselves by it and be imprisoned by our wounds. Or we can find meaning in it, transform our pain to purpose, and take the road less travelled to peace, love, and happiness.

Ultimately, we choose our own way.

***

To contact Dawn:

dawn@thecognitivesoul.com

www.thecognitivesoul.com

www.thecognitivesoul.com/free-discovery-call/

www.facebook.com/cognitivesoul

www.instagram.com/the_cognitive_soul

Deborah Crowe

"Work-Life Fit is not a trend, it's a lifestyle" - Deborah Crowe

As the CEO of a successful medical case management practice for 23 years, Deborah recognized the growing need for further supports for professionals and families dealing with catastrophic illnesses and the need for stress management. Leading with this new vision, Deborah has evolved into a Work-Life Fit Expert and has created a model for revitalization, stress management, and leadership success.

Deborah provides individual life coaching to women, men, and couples and enjoys the diversity of working with companies (small to large) to assist with their Employee Assistance Programs, working with their Human Resources and Disability Management departments to reduce and eliminate short-term disability claims and get employees back to work, happy and healthy! It's all about being the mediator between the employer and employee and offering effective communication.

Each month, Deborah profiles a "Mom of the Month" on Facebook Business Page (https://www.facebook.com/deb.crowe/) with the goal of sharing, educating, and showing women that we all come from different walks of life. Deborah chooses a woman from a different socioeconomic and psychosocial perspective so that other women can relate as we all teach and help each other.

Inspiration Rx: Live Life. Be Yourself

By Deborah Crowe

Inspiration is all around us. Sometimes you may have to look into the corners of your day to find it. It's there I can assure you as each day I find it! I hope this chapter gives you clarity on your life, hope, and a presence of gratitude that we all should have on a daily basis.

Participating in a personal development book series was exhilarating to me. My first exposure to *The Change* Book Series was in Book #5. My chapter was on work-life balance. Book 5 was published in June 2015 and have I been having fun with this publication and my business since last summer! *The Change* Book Series has catapulted my business, my brand, and my network has grown to be global!

The mentoring that I have been given by Jim Britt and Jim Lutes has been incredible. When you are open to receiving, are coachable, and follow through with the strategies that you are being taught, that is a winning scenario for sure and I am living proof!

I really wanted to value add and leave my imprint on *The Change* Book Series. One day while I was having a mentoring call with Jim and Jim, I asked if I could start a radio show. As always, they both asked me what I envisioned. Four weeks later, The Change Book Radio Show aired on Blog Talk Radio. To say this was an exciting time is an understatement. Every Wednesday, we aired live and I would travel the world via the airwaves interviewing the different co-authors from around the globe. 22 countries and over 200 co-authors that were coaches, authors, speakers, and consultants who represented every industry you could imagine! What enticed me was their ability to tell their story. My approach was to live in the moment and not have a show that was staged. I would read their individual chapters within *The Change* Book Series, familiarize myself enough to conduct the interview, and always integrate an element of surprise during their 30-minute segment. As my business got busier, I could no longer maintain hosting the radio show;

however, I was able to elevate it to the iTunes platform, which was also very exciting! Rich Perry and Larunce Pipkin (also fondly known as my Book 5 buddies) took over hosting of the show and it continues to be successful, interesting, and informative each week!

I felt compelled to write another chapter in *The Change* Book Series about the ongoing "change" in my own life. Personal and professional development is and will always be part of my daily regime. We can only get better with ongoing education, embracing change, aging, changing out behavior, and maturity.

Every day, I have the same routine. I wake up and I am grateful that I have another day. The first task of my day is to journal about my gratitude. It sets the tone for my day, it gives me happiness, focus, clarity, and renews my "why" for whom I chose to be and how I live my life. Each day, I give myself a powerful affirmation to challenge myself to grow as a woman, entrepreneur, mother, wife, friend, and overall decent human being.

We live in a technology dependent society. It's easy to be harsh, negative, and complain. If you choose to start your day with gratitude and maintain that mindset for your day, you will be presently surprised how your day will evolve and give you more than you could imagine.

One of my favorite things is walking throughout the day and seeing many strangers. I make a point of saying hello and always giving them a big smile. Consider that you may be the only person that speaks to them for the whole day. A smile is easy to give and it uses lots of muscles in your face and makes you happy!

As a volunteer at our local Hospice, my gratitude for life is immeasurable. It's easy to get caught up in life and forget about what is really important. Firstly, having your health is true wealth in life. Creating memories with your family and friends is what life truly is about. Collecting memories, not things. Many people never figure this out or when they do, it's too late.

When was the last time you made a phone call to a friend you have not spoken to in a while?

Have you ever taken the time to compliment someone for no reason?

How often do you handwrite a card or letter and mail it to someone?

These are not unusual tasks to do; however, we've allowed technology to consume our lives and sometimes it's a nice reminder to return to your roots. The basics of what we were taught from our parents and grandparents. Truly, allowing yourself to live in and embrace the moment.

It's time to let go of the overused term of "work-life balance." The term has been choked and has seriously taken on its own platform. I now love to use the term "work-life fit." We wake up each day. We pause. We give gratitude. We know what we have to do. Life will allow us to ebb and flow. We have to let go of perfection. There is no one who is perfect. We are born to be the best version of ourselves every day. That's it. No complicated story or equation needed.

For the past five years, I have provided coaching, mentoring, and consulting on work-life balance. The common theme that I see in all my private clients and companies that I work with is the need to be validated.

We all need to have a 'why' in our life. We need to have a purpose to serve and feel appreciated. It's basic human nature.

My life is no different than anyone else. I was born in the 60's and the youngest of five children. I was actually the "mistake." My parents were hardworking and extremely dysfunctional together; however, their generation stayed together and did not "air their laundry" and all was fine and good.

Alcohol, drugs, and rock 'n roll were the main three coping strategies in the 60's and 70's and led the way to our household dysfunction. Sitting back as a child, I remember with vivid memories and clarity the social parties my parents would have as they had stature and money and everyone who was associated with my parents in business or in our neighborhood wanted to hang around with my parents. As I reflect back, my parents were mentors and leaders doing the best they could with the tools they had been given.

In my formidable years, I truly was a "loner." For those who know me, they find that shocking. I love people. Networking and socializing come easy for me, yet, I do enjoy time by myself to fall into deep relaxation and practice meditation daily to keep my mind, body, and soul in complete alignment and always know that my creativity continues to growth alongside my passion for learning and new experiences.

I've experienced a lot of loss and trauma in my life. There are days where I feel my experiences are that of a very old person. Often I am asked how I got through some of the experiences. My answer is simple. I gave into the pain and grief and gave myself the time needed and required to bounce back. I also promised myself that the light was always at the end of the tunnel, even though sometimes it was a dim shimmer.

Losing your dad at age 21 is very hard, as you don't have that fatherly figure to lean on. What got me through was my last discussion with my dad before he passed away. He encouraged me to start my own business and to work with people. He recommended that I always be humble and kind and treat others the way I want to be treated. However, he prepared me to experience this many times over my life as a one-way street. My dad also prepared me for jealousy, resentment, and other negative emotional traits that come with success as an entrepreneur. Certainly, a hard lesson to learn as a young adult, however, having the fatherly advice of not engaging or having emotion has served me well and it's not my story. No personal feelings are involved and I move on to the next task at hand. Business is business.

My mother is someone I do not speak of often. We had a very tumultuous relationship and she suffered from mental health and addiction (alcoholism). When I was a young girl, I would often dream and visualize the mother I wanted to be. As human beings, we can certainly "get over" negative aspects in our life with dreaming and visualizing. That is how I made it through my childhood along with hanging on to my hope and surrounding myself with kind people, my faith, self-love, and always telling myself that everything was going to be okay and that I was a good kid and someday would do amazing things with my life.

Today, I am the proud mother of two beautiful daughters. Our relationship is healthy, loving, and we have great respect for each other. Working through the dysfunctional relationship I had with my own mother, knowing that someday I would be the mother that I wanted to have, provided me again with the light at the end of the tunnel and two daughters who I love unconditionally, mentor, and will help to launch to be the best version of who they are meant to be!

People-watching to this day is still one of my favorite activities to do as it's fascinating to me. Communication on all levels, especially non-verbal communication, including body language, hand gestures, eye movement, nervous laughing, etc. is how people act and respond in social situations continues to astonish me. On a deeper level, it's foundationally related to their childhood upbringing along with their life experiences as an adult.

Now that I have reached the wonderful age of 50, it gives me clarity and strength to look back over my life to see the woman I have become. I do not question my strength, tenacity, will to learn, and passion to help, love, and serve others. It has stemmed from my childhood and the morals, core beliefs, and experiences that my life has gifted to me. I will be humble and kind for my entire life and enjoy the true emotion of gratitude and happiness that it gives my mind, body, and soul!

My next venture I have founded is Soul Women on the Go. A one-day women's conference that I will have and host all over the world to celebrate woman who are faith-filled. I will collaborate with co-authors from *The Change* Book Series to bring this globally to touch women from all walks of life. Teaching and mentoring over the course of a day filled with motivation, inspiration, and tools to empower you, bring you to the next level of your greatness, and fill your gratitude cup.

"You can never have too much happy!" –Deborah Crowe
#worklifefit

***

To contact Deb:

Direct: (519) 878-5839

Website: www.debcrowe.com

Twitter: @LetsGetBalanced

Linked In: https://ca.linkedin.com/in/debcrowe

Facebook: https://www.facebook.com/deb.crowe/

Lisa Rimas

Lisa Rimas is an Author, Spiritual Leader, Transformational Expert, and Energy Medicine Practitioner who specializes in supporting women on a spiritual path break through self-limitations and awaken to experiencing life with more joy, freedom, and authenticity. With years of training in transformational coaching, spiritual mentorship, and energy work, she sees to the essence of who you are, lasers in on your truth, and helps you quantum leap into your soul's highest grandest expression of you. She supports men and women in rediscovering their truth, who they are, and why they're here. She's a Spiritual Catalyst eager to show you how to discover your innate gifts and fully utilize them to your highest potential and from a place of authenticity.

Path to Enlightenment

By Lisa Rimas

Sitting in the center of an energy vortex, connecting to Mother Earth and feeling the beauty and love that surrounds me. My heart and soul feel expansion and free to be me in this moment. I know deep levels of truth and wisdom. I feel connected to the essence of who I am and why I'm here. I am thankful for this never-ending journey of self-expansion, knowing deeper truths, creating new realities, and receiving the infinite blessings that continue to manifest. I am deeply honored and inspired to empower others to remember and embrace their own truth.

My life did not always look like this. I had a turbulent childhood that spiraled into my teens and adulthood. I was the best victim on the planet. For many years, I felt lost and lived in fear. I suffered from deep insecurities, anxiety, and depression. From a very young age, I learned lack, separation, disrespect, and judgment. I witnessed dysfunction, deceit, and control. I learned perfectionism. I bought into all the illusions that kept me far from my true self.

From weathering the storms of childhood divorce and all the chaos, manipulation, and confusion that was attached to that—to dating emotionally and unavailable abusive men, being in trouble with the law, and escaping in alcohol, shopping sprees, sex, marijuana, and everything outside of myself in my 20's and 30's. I looked to everything outside of me for validation, instant gratification, and pleasure. My life was a big "mirror" reflecting the waves of emotions I was desperately attempting to escape from—unworthiness, lack of connection, self-doubt, emptiness, and not feeling important. I wanted so deeply to know greater love and purpose, yet I kept attracting people to validate my internal world.

In knowing as an adult and professional success coach that our feelings are only a reflection of our own thinking and not our circumstances, I pause and ask myself, "What meaning did I give my thoughts around my childhood?" When I was a little girl, my dad's visitation rights were revoked and we didn't see one another until I turned 18; about 9 years later. At such a young age, I remember being in court, yet I don't recall the details. I do remember the meaning and energy I gave to it. I felt that my feelings were not important and that I didn't matter. All these unpleasant feelings that I've mentioned shaped my life.

This is where we surrender to believing that all our thoughts are real, not knowing any other way. We get lost and life becomes difficult. At least mine did. My soul was dropped off at the Lost and Found at a very young age and it was over thirty years before I found it again. Thankfully, I learned later that those thoughts we form are not true at all. I made them up and managed to carry all those thoughts and feelings with me throughout most of my adult life. I spiraled downward in a turbulent wild journey, completely lost with an invisible backpack over my shoulders. T & F was embroidered on this backpack; "Thoughts and Feelings." Wherever I went, I carried them with me; *I'm Not Good Enough, I'm Not Lovable, I Don't Matter*. I had given so much meaning to these thoughts that they became my identity. For decades, I mastered self-sabotage. I was an expert at anything and everything that kept me further away from my truth.

Does this feeling of unworthiness feel pretty universal in our world today? The intricate details around my "stories" are not as pertinent as sharing how I unlocked new ways of being that transformed my life and the world around me. As the stories are what kept me stuck, it was my willingness to transcend perceived beliefs and heal my past to remember the joy and love that is my birthright. It has led me to my life today—in that beautiful energy vortex feeling connection, soul alignment, purpose, and true abundance.

Before I was willing to let go of all the false perceptions and experience my life AS joy and love, I conformed to what family and friends expected of me, continuing to put myself last and choose struggle. After reuniting with my father, I had a 12-year successful run working for his company until we had a big disagreement. Not only did that disagreement leave me looking for a new job, we didn't speak for almost a decade. I carried a lot of anger and resentment, which manifested into physical illness. My invisible backpack was getting heavier.

Yet from the outside looking in, people thought I had it made. And I spent a lot of energy keeping up with that perception. I had a 26-year career in sales and enjoyed a luxury lifestyle; healthy salary, huge bonuses, $10k Christmases, shopping sprees, beautiful homes, 5-star restaurants, new cars, fine jewelry, and more vacations a year than some have in a lifetime.

I had what many people in their 20's and 30's dream of, yet my soul was thirsty for more. "What's missing" I intuitively inquired? When I stepped back from all the "stuff," I recognized my soul was craving love and belonging. I was just depleted trying to keep up with the Joneses living a facade. I can recall the whispers of my soul calling out to me—"you are meant for something greater." I didn't know what I was searching for and those heartstrings became fleeting moments. I didn't know how to listen to my intuition back then. I lived inside my head. I was on the hamster wheel of "doing" and "proving" for many years, and the "proving" kept my experience alive, eventually leading to more health issues, severe burnout, and being on the verge of a nervous breakdown in my late 30's.

Throughout it all, I was always in pursuit of happiness. When I was 29, three people in a row told me that Landmark Forum would change your life. My girlfriend, Lisa, and I signed up right away. It was an unbelievable experience, yet I only experienced temporary shifts. In recent years, I trained with some of the best experts in subconscious reprogramming and peak performance, including the private mentorship of Jim Lutes. In 2009, I graduated from iPEC as a professional leadership coach. April of 2013 was my most pivotal turning point. I spent 5 days sharing the space and beautiful energy of 3000 fellow coaches, speakers, and authors at a Suzanne Evans event. I said to myself, "This is how I want to feel from now on. This feels REAL. I feel like ME." It felt surreal simply being an authentic expression of myself. This feeling of connection is what my heart craved, yet the life and environment I created for myself back home was like an outdated version of the life my soul was bursting at the seams to create! The day before my return home, I had a feeling of dread as I thought about going back to my chaotic life. I had a knowingness that I was done with the struggle and I wished to know greater truths. My intuition kicked through every fear I had. I didn't know the "HOW." All I knew was that I was committing to self-love and happiness!

With loving support from my family and the Universe, I took a very bold leap of faith and resigned from my six-figure career to reinvent my life. I flew back home and found renters for my town home in 3 days. Within 45 days, I was driving 1200 miles southbound with Miss Lacie, my loving Maltese, to move to Florida. This was where I dove deeply into the windows of my soul to seek greater truth and love.

Taking ownership was the first step. I took responsibility in perceiving that I wasn't important to my family, for feeling controlled and manipulated, for feeling unloved and abandoned, unheard and not understood. I took responsibility for all of the perceived rejection, need for approval, and for taking on everyone else's shit.

It was in taking ownership that I created the space to *step out of the game* and embark on a magical journey towards enlightenment and spiritual transformation. Nothing could have prepared me for this journey I was about to embark on. I share with deep gratitude that God divinely orchestrated every person, friend, teacher, mirror, mentor, coach healer, opportunity, and situation to support me on my path to awakening.

When I took responsibility for my life and committed to this path of self-love, it also created space for me to see the *gifts* in everything. The gift in being misunderstood gave me the capacity to deeply understand myself and know self-reliance. The gift in feeling like I don't matter gave me the opportunity to open my heart to self-love. The gift in judgment gave me the opportunity to experience acceptance and unconditioned love. The gift in chaos allowed me the capacity to find peace within. The gift in building a suit of armor so no one could hurt me allowed me the opportunity to learn how to trust others and myself. The gift in living a lie was the opportunity to find my way back home and live authentically.

Learning how to receive was the most challenging principle for me to open up to. I was so used to taking care of everyone else. I'm sure many people, especially women, can relate to this. The Art of Receiving invites us to increase our self-worth and value. Whatever we are manifesting in life, whether it be financial prosperity or more confidence, as soon as we *believe* we are worthy of it, we will open up energetic gateways to receive it. This is where healing and expansion occur. I went from not feeling worthy to knowing and experiencing abundance as my divine birthright. It is a daily ritual that I practice to this day.

I committed to breaking down the walls. The Art of Surrender was equally challenging coming from a childhood with a lot of masculine control like energy. Over time, I learned to *let go* and *trust* that there is something greater than me out there. My connection to God and the Universe became fierce and it's what supports me every day. In my surrendering, I learned the principle of moving from force to flow. I recognized that if I'm trying to force something to happen, I'm energetically aligned with not already having it. I mastered where to focus my energy and this is where I began to learn the art of manifestation. It required me to be fierce in standing in my truth and believing in myself. Through mastering my mindset, energy work, private mentorship, healings, affirmations, you name it—I did whatever it took to align with my truth and stay connected to the essence of who I am. I'm sure many of you can relate to this place of truth, soul alignment, and inner freedom. Once mastered, one may experience moments or snippets of illusion and fear, but there's no going backwards.

We all come into this world with our own set of experiences and they are unique to each of us. The soul seeks clarity, truth, and love. It is when we go within to connect to our "inner compass" that we find these hidden treasures of the soul. With my heart wide open to receiving, I learned how to use discernment with my ego-based thoughts, learning that I had choice over what I believed. I learned what was true. If my body felt light and free, that was my truth. If my body felt unease and constriction, that was fear. In each moment, it got easier to realign my thoughts and choose love and truth. I now say hello to the fear, and thanks for stopping by.

In my path to enlightenment, I learned many key spiritual success principles and how to revolutionize the way I live, love, and lead. With gusto, I learned how to master my emotions, relationships, and consciousness. I was guided to teachings around feminine leadership, human potential, healing, belief work, emotional freedom, shadow energy, and too many others to list all of them. The point is that I took responsibility for my own healing and I began to transcend limiting beliefs. I committed to daily self-care rituals. Still today, I practice gratitude, mindfulness, meditation, different energy, and self-healing modalities. I've embraced how to honor my emotions and love whatever rises. I've learned how to invite pain in and ask what it's here to teach me. I've learned how to live on my own terms without feeling guilty. I've learned how to say No. I've learned that no one defines our reality. No, not even my parents. (Thank you for being my greatest teachers!) Life is going to test us at times. When we live a heart-centered life, we need to be able to look at others and ourselves and say, "I'm afraid, and I'm also worthy of love, belonging, and joy." Because you are!

These fundamental spiritual success principles are not taught in school. Taking 100% responsibility for your life and your results is first and foremost. This creates beautiful openings for new awareness and new truths to birth. When you release the negativity, it creates space for what you do want in your life. Choose your surroundings wisely. Use joy as your internal GPS!

I also invite you to embrace the ego. The ego can be useful. It's that part of us that we can say, "Okay, I'm going to retrain you to serve my soul and higher purpose." When your personality comes to serve the energy of your soul, this is when you're in alignment. The intellect, the body, the emotions, the intuition—they all have to be in alignment to truly thrive!

I'll share a perfect example around how I was tested to stay in alignment recently. A few weeks ago after a morning walk with my dog Lacie, she became very ill. She was vomiting a yellow liquid and became very lethargic. She wouldn't move. I'm comfortable with intuitively saying that something poisonous or toxic was ingested. She's only 5 pounds, so naturally I was initially scared. I swiftly picked her up to take her to the vet. On our drive in, I called in our God team and began praying out loud in gratitude, "I am so grateful for the miracles unfolding in Lacie's health and healing right now. Thank you God for your presence." Repeat. Repeat. Repeat—until we got to the vet.

All the rooms are filled with patients, yet the doctors are all in my line of sight as I walk into the door. They take Lacie in the back to assist her right away. A few minutes pass and the receptionist comes out to talk to me. As she begins speaking, she starts crying. "It's serious." My entire world went blank for about five seconds. Then she quickly proceeds to apologize for her emotions. She was crying because she lost her dog last week that looks just like Lacie. Wow! I felt the sacred space I'm creating for complete healing be truly tested in that moment. I felt every cell of my DNA fighting back like a fierce warrior woman. I was not taking on her fears and pain. I sent her and the entire vet love & light and shifted my energy to be an open channel for only light and healing to occur.

Within 15 minutes of that scenario, another tech says to me, "Oh no, I wonder if Lacie was sprayed by one of those frogs? That could kill a dog Lacie's size." I felt my entire body tingle. And knowing what I know about the subconscious mind, I immediately released all her beliefs & fears around that and everything that did not align with Infinite Truth, Love, and Healing for Lacie AND myself. I felt it all melt away like a beautiful rainfall. I cleared my schedule and went home to pray. I remained in complete alignment with miracles unfolding and seeing Lacie strong, happy, and healthy. I was in utter peace surrounded by the presence of divine love. It was surreal. I felt all the prayers from loved ones. My dear sister, Fiona Mauchlan, was guided to work on Lacie remotely. She's a powerful pet healer. The doctors were surprised how quickly Lacie bounced back, only needing to be on oxygen for about 30 minutes and she was back to her happy sassy bouncy self in a short time. One of the techs made a comment about God working through her. I thought to myself. "YES"! What a beautiful sign!

While more miracles unfolded, I feel guided to share this. This scenario is extreme and my experience is MY experience, not yours. It can be as simple as manifesting love in your life. When we are being *intentional and clear* on a specific outcome or desire, I encourage you to stay energetically aligned & authentically open to that Truth being actualized. Remain open to receive those blessings that are ALREADY there.

I am grateful to share that in my own healing journey, I've been able to heal and positively shift the relationship I have with my biological father for the first time in 47 years. This is truly a gift! I am blessed to have an amazing tribe of truth seekers and sisters whom I journey and change lives with! Sharing one another's unique journey's allowed me to see the beautiful qualities within me on a deeper level and gave me permission to be ME. They have born witness as I embraced a more loving and meaningful relationship with myself, the most loving gift of all. I feel safe, supported, loved, inspired, confident, and deeply fulfilled. I'm grateful to have arrived at what I call my *Sweet Spot*. I continue to make my mess my message by supporting other women who wish to heal, transform, and awaken.

Choose Love!! Choose Truth!!

***

To Contact Lisa:

Website: www.LisaRimas.com

Blog: www.FreeToBeMeWithLisaMarie.com

Dr. Shahid Sheikh

Dr. Shahid Sheikh has been consulting internationally since 1987, and coaching professionally since 2013—and has loved just about every minute of it! With over 40 years of progressive management and leadership experience, he now helps high-impact executives, business owners, and entrepreneurs succeed in their careers and achieve exceptional business results through effective-leadership.

In addition to a Doctorate in Organization Change, he is also certified at the ACC level by the ICF (International Coach Federation).

Case Study: Critical Areas Leaders Must Practice in the 21st Century to be Effective

By Dr. Shahid Sheikh

The following is a case study of a young male CEO who attained rapid promotion through sheer hard work. Oscar (pseudonym) soon found that though he was a high-impact performer, technically excellent, broadly talented, and enthusiastic about his new roles; however, he had limited management and leadership skills and experience, and importantly, most importantly had not developed vital people management skills.

The firm's cofounder, who had initially recruited Oscar, decided to retire and hired a leadership transition coach to find his replacement. After an extensive search, the coach recommended Oscar for the position.

Oscar's direct reports were predominantly industry veterans, older, had more tenure with the company, and were resentful of Oscar's promotion. His indirect reports were younger, fresh out of college Millennials. Within six months of his appointment as CEO, the West Coast office was in chaos.

Therein began the problem. Revenues dropped significantly and employees began to leave.

The cofounder brought me in as the leadership development coach to assess and remedy the situation. To identify the issues, I interviewed the staff individually and used three assessment instruments.

First, I would like to briefly catalogue the changes in 20th Century vs. 21st Century Leadership and why it is critical to embrace new skills to become an effective leader.

The demographic changes—the exodus of baby boomers in leadership positions into retirement—are making developing effective leadership bench strength an even greater challenge for organizations to resolve in order to remain competitive in the future.

Effective leadership in the 21st Century requires a complex and varied portfolio of leadership competencies such as driving for business results, working with others, building effective groups, and technological proficiency, etc. Twenty-first century leaders also need enhanced cognitive skills and abilities, such as communicating effectively, problem solving, interpersonal skills, skills in human relations, teamwork, decisiveness and tenacity, and ability to develop organizational capabilities.

Mark David Nevins and Stephen Stumpf, in *21st Century Leadership: Redefining Management Education,* wrote, "The most successful leaders in the 21st Century effectively manage multiple points of view simultaneously and empathize with all stakeholders in order to develop people." The authors added that the common characteristics of these effective leaders are focused on the intangible aspects of an organization. These leaders are effectively leading people with self-leadership, authenticity, integrity, honesty, and accountably, simultaneously developing relationships and promoting collaboration and teamwork.

However, most business leaders today are stuck in the old leadership model: organizational hierarchies influenced by two World Wars and the Depression, and structured along military lines, with multilayered structures to establish control through rules and processes.

In the past, people climbed the ranks in search of power, status, money, and privileges that came with rank. **However, things are different now**. The hierarchical model simply no longer works. Bill George, in *The New 21st Century Leaders,* wrote, "During the last half of the 20th century, business leadership became an elite profession, dominated by managers who ruled their enterprises from the top down."

Effective leaders focused on internal and external stakeholders are replacing hierarchical leaders who focus on serving short-term shareholders.

Preproposal and Solution

Organizational assessment measures seven critical areas identified by NIST and Criteria for Performance Excellence as used in the Baldrige National Quality Program. The Performance

Excellence framework includes leadership, strategic planning, customer and market focus, human resource focus, process management, and business results categories.

The personality assessment instrument (ADVanced Insight) identifies what natural talents the individual possesses based on how he or she thinks and makes decisions, why he or she is motivated to use them based on his or her motivators, cofounders, and drivers, and how the individual prefers to use them based on his or her preferred behavioral style.

The Social + Emotional Intelligence Profile Instrument identifies an individual's social and emotional intelligence strengths and development opportunities. The Profile measures the 26 competencies identified as critical in socially and emotionally intelligent individuals, families, teams, and organizations.

Collectively from the assessment outcomes and personal interviews, I gathered that Oscar's tendencies were to appear right in front of others; failure to ask for help; competing with others instead of cooperating; exaggerating his own value and contribution; setting unrealistic, overly ambitious and unattainable goals for himself and others; etc. Oscar's profile also indicated the tendency to push himself hard, often at the expense of others. In addition, the reports profiled Oscar's tendencies to micromanage and take over instead of delegating ("if you want it done right..."), taking credit for others' efforts, blaming others for mistakes, inability to admit mistakes, and resistance to accept feedback or criticism.

I found that Oscar's interpersonal skills were often abrasive and his leadership style was militaristic and hierarchical, based on the titles and ranks and the perceived power and authority that suited his own personal style, as described by Charles de Gaulle, the French Army General who said, "Men are of no importance. What counts is who commands." Oscar's leadership style in essence was top down. He was unable to engage his employees' hearts and souls, thus rendering him ineffective.

In essence, Oscar's leadership style was hierarchical, managing the organization from the top down and controlling through rules and processes influenced by his rank, perceived power, and status.

Collectively, we discerned that the hierarchical model simply no longer works and Oscar must learn to focus on sustaining superior performance by aligning people around mission and values and empowering leaders at all levels, while concentrating on serving customers and collaborating throughout the organization.

Through discussions, we agreed that effective leaders are passionate about a cause and possess a compelling vision. Effective leaders practice and promote self-leadership with authenticity and display high integrity, honesty, and accountably. Effective leaders develop relationships and promote collaboration and teamwork. They are effective communicators who inspire and motivate with empathy. Effective leaders align organizational mission, vision, and values to individual's goals and values. They are aware of themselves and others, successfully manage their emotions and leadership capacity, and grow and motivate people to develop and attain their potential while fulfilling organizational and personal goals and objectives with determination and empathy. Effective leaders analyze issues and take initiative to solve problems with a strategic perspective.

Oscar and I customized a leadership and team development program focused on authentic and self-leadership, integrity and accountability, and how to inspire and motivate. Oscar agreed that effectively communicating the organizational mission, vision, and values is critical to being an effective leader; as such, effective communication should be integrated in his developmental plan. Additionally, the developmental plan included setting goals and integrating the process that drives results. Oscar also wanted to learn how to build relationships with his staff and promote teamwork. He also wanted to learn how to recognize and manage effectively his own emotions and his staff's emotions. Finally, we decided to work on becoming aware of communication circumstances, setting and keeping boundaries, leading by asking questions, asking what if questions, and exploring and managing polarity.

The implementation process emphasized the following eight critical areas effective leaders must practice and involved in-person sessions, reading, journaling, team discussions about self-interest and personal gain, and how to push for the best for others by doing best for those they lead and following key essential topics.

Self-Leaderships with Authenticity

I believe the center of leadership is the person who, more than anything else, makes the difference. To lead people effectively and organizations successfully, leaders must first learn to lead themselves. Ken Blanchard notes, "You can't lead others if you can't lead yourself, and you can't lead yourself without the right tools." Leadership success or failure begins with how leaders approach self-leadership.

Effective leadership begins with self-leadership. Bryant and Kazan, in *Self-Leadership*: *How to Become a More Successful, Efficient, and Effective Leader from the Inside Out,* wrote, "Self-leadership is the practice of intentionally influencing your thinking, feeling and behaviors to achieve your objective[s]." Simply stated, self-leadership is having a developed sense of who you are and what you can do, coupled with the ability to influence your communication, emotions, and behaviors on the way to getting there. However, it is not as easy as it sounds. Dee Hock suggests, "We should invest 50 per cent of our leadership amperage in self-leadership and the remaining 50 per cent should be divided into leading down, leading up and leading laterally."

Oscar and I worked on increasing his ability to acknowledge, understand, and be conscious of his values, perspectives, strengths, and weaknesses. Next, we worked on his ability to nurture and harness his passion, abilities, emotions, and leadership, and capacity in decision making. We also focused on improving his social awareness, which is the ability to acknowledge and recognize the passion, gifts, strengths, weaknesses, potential, and needs of others. Finally, we worked on relationship management, which is the ability to grow and motivate other people to develop their potential and fulfill the organization's objectives.

Integrity, Honesty, and Accountably

Integrity is doing the right thing in a reliable way. Of all the facets of character, Zenger and Folkman, in *Making Yourself Indispensable: The Power of Personal Accountability,* write that integrity is the most critical facet that builds valuable trust between people. Leaders with integrity are authentic, consistent, accountable, and lead by example. Integrity is often equated with courage and doing things right for the company.

Kouzes and Posner, in *The Leadership Challenge,* wrote that honesty is essential to a leader's legitimacy, credibility, and ability to develop trust with followers. It is about being fair, truthful, sincere, transparent, and open and various other aspects of moral character, such as keeping your word, following through on promises, and delivering on time.

Accountability is willingness to take responsibility and ownership for one's behavior and actions. Eisenhower once said, "I know only one method of operation. To be as honest with others as I am with myself." It indicates positive and virtuous attributes such as integrity, truthfulness, and straightforwardness.

Hendricks and Ludeman, in *The Corporate Mystic,* write that leaders with integrity are authentic with themselves and others. They "walk-the-talk"; doing the things they said they would do.

Leaders with integrity ignore self-interest and personal gain, pursue the best for others by doing best for those they lead, and protect the organization's resources. Leaders with integrity always keep their people in mind. They constantly look for ways to do better for their people and take responsibility to do a better job as a leader, by leading by example.

We worked on gaining the trust and respect of his direct and indirect reports, by being open and honest and maintaining integrity. Oscar also worked on sticking to his values; no matter what the outside pressures, stresses, or temptations are. He focused on honest dealings, predictable reactions, fair judgements, and controlling his emotions.

Empathy and Emotional Intelligence

Emotional intelligence is a critical requirement of leadership. Daniel Goleman, in his article "What makes a Leader," stated, "The most effective leaders are alike in one crucial way: they all have a high degree of what has come to be known as emotional intelligence." He argues that it is not that IQ and technical skills are irrelevant. They do matter, but…they are the entry-level requirements for executive positions. Recent research and studies clearly show that emotional intelligence is the prerequisite of leadership. Without it, a person can have the best training in the world, an incisive, analytical mind, and an endless supply of smart ideas, but he still will not make a great leader.

The self-leadership development plan for Oscar focused on the four cornerstone of emotional intelligence to improve his self-leadership potential: self-awareness, self-management, social awareness, and relationship management and included understating and practicing the concepts of self-awareness and self-regulation to improve his self-leadership potential, and empathy for others and his social skills, and proficiency in managing relationships and building networks.

Oscar's developmental plan included a two-step process of journaling and observing: (1) his own values, perspectives, strengths, weaknesses, leadership tendencies, and emotional needs, focusing and managing his emotions, his leadership abilities and capacity in decision making; and (2) the needs of others and his ability to grow and motivate other people.

Communicate Powerfully and Effectively

Effective communication is skillful, clear, concise, open, transparent, and easily understandable by others, and critical to effective leadership. Gallup found that engagement is highest among employees who have some form of daily communication about their roles and responsibilities, but also about what happens in their lives outside work.

Effective leaders realize that words have power and communicate in multiple ways, verbally, nonverbally, and in written form, and combine their communication skills with other essential leadership traits. Effective leaders are never in sending mode only. They understand the power of listening and receiving communication is just as important as asking questions instead of sending top-down orders. Effective leaders realize asking more and telling less builds a relationship of mutual trust.

Effective leaders lead by asking better questions to help build positive relationships. Edgar Schein, in *Humble Inquiry: The Gentle Art of Asking Instead of Telling,* argues that we live in a world that believes our role as professionals is to "fix and tell" rather than "listen and inquire." Effective leaders practice the art of inquiring and asking questions instead of telling the supposed answers. "Humble inquiry is the fine art of drawing someone out, of asking questions, to which you do not already know the answers, of building a relationship based on curiosity and interest in the other person," Schein wrote. He argues that telling "puts the person down."

Oscar worked on techniques such as opening the lines of communication, communicating diplomatically and tactfully in a variety of tough situations such as interpersonal conflicts and departmental infighting, conducting result-focused meetings, the importance of focusing on the issue and not the person, etc.

Inspire and Motivate Others

Charismatic leaders are effective and very skilled communicators. Charismatic leaders attract and influence others to achieve remarkable outcomes. However, I contend that to inspire and motivate others, leaders need to be much more than just charismatic. Effective leaders have to be visionary, principled, enthusiastic, optimistic, and driven. They do not have to be technical experts in their vision; they surround themselves with, inspire, and motivate others who are technical experts.

Inspirational leaders give and receive honest feedback, influence and motivate others by walking-the-talk, by becoming the role model doing what they said they would, and by setting examples. Effective leaders are humble and they lead by asking humble questions. They invest in their people's well-being and often ask them about it. Employees value communication from their manager not just about their roles and responsibilities, but also about what happens in their lives outside of work. A Gallup study revealed that employees who feel as though their manager is invested in them, as people, are more likely to be engaged.

Oscar worked on becoming aware of his team members' personal situations and showing genuine concern for their well-being, practicing appropriate appreciation and encouragement, setting good examples, and giving feedback. Oscar was able to win over his team members by making them feel comfortable talking about any subject, whether it is work related or not.

Setting Attainable Goals and Drive for Results

Employee performance begins with leadership. Effective leaders are adept at establishing challenging and achievable performance goals and driving for improving organizational performance by supporting individuals' achievements and personal growth and holding them accountable.

Oscar's developmental plan included using SMART Goals protocol. The SMART acronym comprises Specific, Measureable, Achievable, Realistic, and Time-Bound. We included all team members in setting performance-specific organizational and personal goals, which were specifically defined, communicated, and understood by all team members. They understood and agreed the goals were important and understood why their performance was critical to their own and the organization's success.

During the planning process, team members ensured and agreed that the goals were measurable and attainable. The process included written reports at the end of each week.

Align Organizational Mission, Vision, and Values to Individuals' Goals and Values

Effective leaders realize the key to helping employees feel positively about their work is aligning the organizational mission, vision, and values to individuals' goals and values, and that communicating that vision to employees, making it part of their day-to-day activities, helps employees see and understand the impact of their work.

Larry Myler, in *Strategy 101: It's All about Alignment,* writes that aligning organizational mission, vision, values, and meaningful purpose to individuals' goals, values, and purpose reinforces and gives an organization a major advantage because everyone has a clear sense of what to do at any given time. Effective leaders who align organizations and their own vision into viable strategies and goals lead to organizational and individual success.

Effective leaders, according to Amabile and Kramer in *The Progress Principle,* nurture their employees' inner work lives by allowing them to make progress in meaningful work.

Oscar worked with his team members to envision and define a common future, creating a strategy, focusing on their company's competitive advantage, communicating change on how they have been conducting and setting targets to bring their organization's vision and strategy into every team member's daily work.

Build Relationships, Develop Others, Collaborate, and Promote Teamwork

Building relationships is one of the strongest skill sets related to leadership effectiveness. Effective leaders collaborate and get along with others. Relationships and collaboration are essential, but neither negates the need for strong leadership. Angela Ahrendts, retail chief at Apple, said, "Everyone talks about building a relationship with your customer. I think you build one with your employees first."

Effective leaders realize that the measure of their effectiveness lies in the results achieved by inspiring others and by embracing and nurturing the need for relationships and collaboration. Speaker of the House of Representatives Sam Rayburn's advice to a young Lyndon Johnson was, "If you want to get along, go along!"

In *Great Leaders Build Off Great Relationships,* John Baldoni writes that an effective leader thus must be able to build relationships and create communities of practice, actions, and values. These communities provide opportunities to network and to become involved with others who share like values. To quote Peter F. Drucker: "Every enterprise requires commitment to common goals and shared values." Leaders look to these values as the basis for action. Values are important ideals that guide our priorities and are core to an organization. Values tie people together, set vision, and affect what we do as organizations and communities.

In his book *Leadership and the Culture of Trust*, Gilbert Fairholm wrote, "In reality, leadership is an expression of collective, community action. True leadership describes unified action of leaders and followers (stakeholders) working together to jointly achieve mutual goals. It is collaborative." Collaboration is what happens in any organization or community. How well is it done depends on how well the leader promotes and nurtures collaboration and teamwork.

Oscar promoted collaboration and teamwork by asking questions, really listening, developing a mutual commitment, and supporting their decisions. He realized this goal by making sure that his expectations were clear and understood, and by communicating that the outcome(s) will benefit everyone. Oscar communicated his support, established the ground rules, and clarified goals and expectations. He also involved the staff to organize the process.

Outcome

At the 12-month mark, to measure the outcome(s), I interviewed the staff members individually and used the same three assessment instruments.

I found that Oscar's interpersonal skills showed a significant improvement, and his leadership style had become more empowering and served his staff and team members at all levels of their collective and individual accountabilities. Oscar's scores on individual assessments showed noticeable improvements in self-leadership, behavioral self-control, situational awareness, and coaching and mentoring others. His teamwork and collaboration scores did not show a significant improvement, which can be attributed to the nature of a business that is monthly quota, and bottom-line driven. In organizational assessment, his staff members felt the he was significantly open, approachable, and demonstrated integrity and accountability. They also agreed that his actions inspired and motivated them. According to the results in organizational assessment, he had effectively communicated and they had a better understanding of the organizational mission, vision, and values.

Additionally, Oscar, with the help of managerial staff, had an incremental development plan for each individual staff member, which included setting goals and integrating the process that drives for results. The most significant improvement discerned from the assessment outcomes was that Oscar was able to recognize and effectively manage his own emotions and his staff members' emotions.

In twelve months, Oscar transformed himself from being an ineffective leader to an effective leader by improving his leadership style and his interpersonal skills to their full potential. He had learned to become aware of communication circumstances, was able to set goals and keep boundaries, led by asking questions, and asked what if questions, etc.

To have a meaningful conversation and a free 30-minute consultation on how he can help you or upcoming leaders in your organization:

Call: 310.928.3501

Make an appointment: https://drshahidsheikh.youcanbook.me/

Email: drshahidsheikh@significantconsulting.net

Connect on LinkedIn: www.linkedin.com/in/shahidsheikh

Visit: significantconsulting.net

Evelyn J. Waterhouse

Evelyn Waterhouse is passionate about people who desire healthy and sustainable relationships. Evelyn Waterhouse's discovery of an authentic joy in working with people led her to develop The Amazing Company. With insight gleaned from extensive research into human behavior, she consistently provides transcendent interpersonal experiences. Identifying the needs of each person readily sets them at ease with her abundant enthusiasm and winning smile. Evelyn's values are Peace, Love, Heart, and Joy.

Evelyn's core belief is that Leadership originates and ends at home. Coaching men and women in valuing, not only themselves as individuals, but also their spouses, children, extended family and friends. Recognizing how you lead your family will set the standard of how you take the lead in the world.

Evelyn has developed a Building Healthy Relationship program for people who wish to understand what a healthy relationship is and what it is not.

Evelyn holds the Associate Certified Coach (ACC) designation from the International Coach Federation. Her volunteerism has been acknowledged with awards from the Hon. Rob Nicholson MP and Wayne Gates MPP. At the municipal level, she received the Good Citizen Award.

Learning to Love from the Inside

By Evelyn Waterhouse

What is love and how do we know when we have found it? For those of you that have been blessed with a healthy and harmonious lifestyle, which include self-love, loving your work, and a healthy committed relationship; I commend and congratulate you. For those of us that are in the process of understanding what needs to change within ourselves, this chapter is for you.

> *"What is necessary to change a person is to change his awareness of himself." -Abraham Maslow*

Asking the hard questions for those of us that are in search of love will find the answers from within. Who, what, when, where, or why of what you do. Are you looking for the whole package, a person who possesses all the qualities that we seek; a beautiful face, a great body, intelligence, humor, kindness, confidence, financial stability, maturity, integrity? Before seeking those which you desire in others, ask yourself; are you the whole package for someone else? Holding one's self to the standards that they seek in others is a true reflection of knowing and honoring that you have the power to change not only yourself, but the people you surround yourself with, and the environment you are in. The best love is the one that makes you a better person, without changing you into someone other than who you are.

"Say not, 'I have found the truth,' but rather, 'I have found a truth.'

Say not, 'I have found the path of the soul.' Say rather, 'I have met the soul walking upon my path.'

For the soul walks upon all paths.

The soul walks not upon a line, neither does it grow like a reed.

The soul unfolds itself like a lotus of countless petals." *Kahlil Gibran*

Love Yourself

We all have heard the words "you must love yourself before you can love someone else." I believe there is more to it than that. It is essential for you to be in a place of total acceptance of who you are and not what others want you to be. Accept the essence of you. Say to yourself every morning, "you are fundamentally a good person and what makes you unique is the source of that goodness." Furthermore, you are worthy of being loved by others, and perhaps more important, you are worthy of loving someone else. Loving your self is all encompassing, your mind (wisdom), body, heart, and spirit.

Wisdom

Open your mind to the experiences of others. Each story they share with you is an opportunity for you to learn in minutes what took them months, years, or even a lifetime. Use your mind to absorb the intelligence, humor, kindness, integrity, and fairness of humanity. You can find it in the world around you; seek it. Love learning and if you don't, learn how. All one needs to do is embrace each lesson rather than look upon it as a chore. Have an open mind and accept that you are capable of learning and growing. *Want* to make changes, then love your mind that has been given to you to use. Be creative, innovative, obtain knowledge, absorb intelligence, see life's silliness, share kindness, and live in integrity for the fairness of humanity.

Body

Yes, most of us would like to be something different, a little taller, and a little thinner, have straight hair or curly hair, or just simply *have* hair. Love the body you have been given. In this day and age of advancement in cosmetic surgery, not only are we capable to alter our facial features, we can change our sex. Life is peaceful when you come to accept what is and loving that amazingly beautiful person right there in the mirror. Just drop the façade! Be authentic;

embrace every part of you, including your body. With this confidence, others will be drawn to you that might otherwise have ignored you. In a word, have a harmonious relationship between your inner self and your outer shell.

Heart

When you see someone you love, your heart skips a beat. Likewise, when you see your loved one hurt, your heart hurts with them. Joy and sorrow come from the same place—your heart. We call what triggers your heart, emotions. These emotions affect your physical well-being every day; this has been confirmed with contemporary science that negative emotions and attitudes can make you ill. If left unchecked, the results can be devastating for your health. Therefore, it is in your best interest to learn to recognize and control your emotions. Intercepting negative emotion and attitudes with positive ones is a great place to start. Self-talk is that voice in your head which we either listen to or ignore. Preventing your self-talk from continuing its objective of negative emotions (anger, fear, not enough, less than) and replacing them with positive self-talk (joy, happiness, abundance, more than) will create shifts for you to gain awareness of where your heart truly wishes to go. Feel your heart, to harmonize with your brain and feel the rhythm of its beat; when your heart and your head match, you are at peace.

Spirit

The human spirit incorporates our passion, creativity, innovation, intellect, emotions, and fears. The human spirit is a piece of human psychology, the arts, philosophy, and knowledge. The human spirit is regarded as the higher element of human nature, such as the collective human spirit of the Civil Rights Movement of the 1960s. Dr. Martin Luther King and other leaders of his time embraced the collective human spirit of freedom for all humans regardless of race, social status, or sexual orientation. Surrounding yourself with people, places, and things that inspire your spirit to grow and flourish, and for others of like minds to come together with awareness, insight, and understanding is the objective at hand. Love your spirit, honor it, and others will seek you out.

Be aware that in the pursuit of these changes, you will be faced with obstacles and challenges to test your willingness to keep moving forward toward your goals. In spite of these challenges, do not fail to assert your freedom of choice and be committed to loving yourself and creating that harmonious state with your mind, body, heart, and spirit.

Love Your Partner

> *"Love one another, but make not a bond of love:*
>
> *Let it rather be a moving sea between the shores of your souls.*
>
> *Fill each other's cup but drink not from one cup.*
>
> *Give one another of your bread but eat not from the same loaf*
>
> *Sing and dance together and be joyous, but let each one of you be alone,*
>
> *Even as the strings of a lute are alone though they quiver with the same music"*
>
> *Kahlil Gibran*

Loving someone else is a very beautiful thing, after saying that what is even more beautiful is the acceptance of someone else for who they are and not what we *want* them to be. You can never change anyone. Top Executive Coach Marshall Goldsmith will tell you, "Is there anything I can do to convince anyone that change is good for them? Nothing! If they don't care, don't waste your time."

So, regardless if you are in a committed relationship or looking to be in one, be mindful of whom you are and what it is that you need in the relationship. Creating a strong foundation that encompasses your core values will guide you in the right direction of what you give and receive from the relationship. Taking the time to know what you value is a great place to start. You can't live something you don't know; dig deep and set it straight. Your core values will be what will guide you in creating the healthy relationship you are seeking in every decision, be it physical, romantic, or financial.

Healthy relationships start with a healthy you. Are you in a place of self-love, and acceptance of who you are and to share that with another, without the need to change? Loving your partner will encompass the mind, body, heart, and soul with the understanding of *how they make you feel*.

Wisdom

Your partner is a separate human being with their own experiences and knowledge. Open your mind and see the person in front of you as a valuable source of wisdom. Do not let yourself devalue their input because of familiarity. Turning towards each other by way of emotional connection through communication will strengthen your relationship or end it. The willingness to see each other as two independent people that wish to share an interdependent relationship is the only way to create and maintain a healthy us. Most relationships are one sided and one person controls the power over the other; in healthy relationships, the husband and wife (or partner) will resist power struggles and treat each other with respect in the decision-making process.

Body

Looking to your partner as a purely physical entity is doing him/her a disservice. Any one of us can change our physical self either by choice or by unfortunate events. It is human nature to like what you see; this is normal, but one must ask himself or herself, is that the only reason you are with this person? Having the ability to see beyond the physical is where you will create intimacy. The physical intimacy that you seek will unfold naturally without shame or trepidation.

Heart

Opening your heart to love puts you in a vulnerable position. It takes courage to say to someone "I love you." There is no fear in love; we fear the vulnerability, the potential of rejection or worse, betrayal in the future. Expressing to your partner that he/she is worthy of your honor and respect with the use of positive language and focusing on the positive qualities that your partner possesses will create a sustainable and loving relationship. This is not to say that we should overlook damaging or destructive behaviors in the name of love. Loving the heart of your partner is with the understanding that each of us is responsible for our own actions, reactions, and the deeds that we perform. Taking ownership of how you make each other feel through your words, behaviors, and habits creates positive shared feelings towards each other, through the use of humor, affection, positive attention, romance, and a great sex life, you feel the heart of your partner and the connection you both create.

Spirit

To own one's spirit is to free them of what society has determined what is normal or right. Whether that is with your religious believes, family culture, or your society at large. Loving the spirit of your partner is the greatest gift you can give to them. Healthy relationships embrace the shared purpose of all members to be free to be whatever they wish to be. Supporting your partner in their purpose in life creates trust and intimacy with an open dialogue for you to share your purpose and passion. It also makes a couple aware of their deepest insecurities. Healthy couples use their time as an opportunity to overcome these insecurities, rather than prey upon them when the going gets tough. The openness to speak freely about your dreams and passion is not with the intention that they must be each other's dreams, but that they are heard and supported by the other. Sincerely supporting the spirit of your partner with extended family, friends, or out in your community with encouraging and inspiring your partner in their world views, vocation, or politics connects you beyond the walls of your home. Keep in mind we are free to agree to disagree. Having said that, what are your deal breakers? One has the free will to honor your own morals and values, the expectation that it is your partner's duty to support opposing different levels of integrity, honesty, or moral standing goes against self-love. Once you have arrived in this state of harmony, you will seldom drain a partner with either unnecessary over-indulgence of attention, gratification, or criticism. Balance is created within the relationship, a balance of respect, mindful language (fighting fair), kindness and caring, open communication, listening, healing, and reconnecting.

Love What You Do

> *"Always you have been told that work is a curse and labor a misfortune.*
>
> *But I say to you that when you work you fulfill a part of earth's furthest dream, assigned to you when that dream was born.*
>
> *And in keeping yourself with labor you are in truth loving life.*
>
> *And to love life through labor is to be intimate with life's inmost secret."*
>
> Kahlil Gibran

To work with love and to love your work are two different things. Not everything in life is enjoyable. I will share with you I am not a big fan of cleaning the bathroom. After saying that, doing the work with love, and with music playing, I am able to love life through labor and work with love for the finished product and the accomplishment of getting the job done.

To love your work and to be focused and true with a sense of ease in which you perform is an amazing thing to behold. The musician with his guitar, the speaker at the podium, the chef with his ingredients, whatever it is that you embrace, it will be of second in nature. The 10, 20, 30 years in which you needed to learn, question, relearn with an open mind with more questions is the origin in which this flawless performance begins.

Mind

Your mind will be in constant alignment with the pursuit of your work. Everything you read, talk, think, will be about *it*. You are on auto pilot and you can't get enough. You want to surround yourself with people who embrace *it*. Having the focus, discipline of doing the undesirable to get you where you want to go. Going back to school to obtain credentials, you learn to face your fears and overcome your insecurities. You want to challenge your natural gifts and improve on them. You want to make changes to fully embrace the love of *it* for how it makes you feel.

Body

Your body will be a state of alignment and ready for you. You will find you are not sick because your mind and body are together working for you and not against you to help you reach your goals and passion. You want to feel healthy so you work out. You want to feel awake so you sleep. You want to be alert so you are mindful of alcohol consumption or drug use. You want to be physically healthy so you eat healthy food.

Heart

Your heart will be in a state of openness and ready for you. The words, thoughts, and ideas will come through from your heart. It will make you feel alive with excitement and fear with dread.

Spirit

Your spirit is the essence of who you are as a person. The understanding that not everything we do in our work life is fun. Work is not hard—we make it hard by way of our attitude towards it. Having an engaging attitude about the mundane or routine creates an opportunity for creativity and innovation. Utilizing your spirit of gratitude towards your work life is with the attitude that to be engaged is not with the intention that my work is hard; rather I am grateful for the opportunity, enthusiasm, and joy of being alive.

Gratefulness and Giving Back

"See first that you yourself deserve to be a giver, and an instrument of giving.

For in truth it is life that gives unto life while you, who deem yourself a giver, are but a witness

And you receivers... and you are all receivers... assume no weight of gratitude, lest you lay a

yoke upon yourself and upon him who gives."

Kahlil Gibran

When you have a greater understanding that life is a balance of emotions, senses of amazement, and seeing the world through the eyes of a child, you have reached a grounded sense of happiness and satisfaction with life, not what life has done for you, but what have you done for your life. When you have the capability of being opportunity centered, everything in life is an opportunity, and not a problem; you can think independently and not be influenced by societal norms, religious norms, or cultural norms. Exploring your sense of humor, not to be mocking or spiteful, rather to be life-affirming, with a concern of the deeper questions in life: What is my purpose? How can I give back? Who am I? Where do I belong?

Having the capability to show calmness and restraint in adversity with the understanding it is not about me; on the contrary, it is how I responsd to what is around me. We are all one in the human race and to feel a deep sense of similarity for humanity with the understanding we need love and acceptance to be truly free.

Sharing the love that you have for yourself is by sharing that love with your spouse, your children (if you are blessed with children), and with extended family and friends. You can only give away what you already have inside of you. Search your love with openness and caring, compassion and understanding; all it takes is an honest smile from your eyes. NO words are needed; you will say everything you need to say through your eyes. Love is how you make someone feel, at home, at work, or out in your community. Be mindful of how you treat others and how others are treating you; life is not hard, we make it hard through our actions, reactions, and the deeds that we perform.

You are amazing at any time in your life.

***

To Contact Evelyn:

www.iamamazing.ca

evelyn@iamamazing.ca

905-658-0236

José Aarão de Andrade

Jose Andrade is an entrepreneur and a life changer; he can connect and build trust with anyone. He works with world leaders and influential people that want to achieve an "impossible" dream/vision. After going through an in-depth process of updating his paradigms, he learned that it is possible to achieve what many would say is impossible, that the power of words manifests one's world. His work involves deep conversations and being able to lead people to enter their world of impossibilities, creating great things that are life changing either for the person in front of him or for those whose life that person will impact.

"To create peace, you have to have it inside yourself. You can only give what you have."

If they told you that what you want is impossible, it is up to you to agree or run for your dreams.

He is committed to creating world peace by creating internal peace, one person at a time.

Presence + Deep Connection + Powerful Vision = Create the Impossible.

How are you showing up in life?
Speak, breathe, and embody what you want as if you already have it.

By José Aarão de Andrade

It was September of 2009; we had been married for only four months and were happy. My wife started having some pain in her chest and told me about it, to which I replied: "That might be because you have been working a lot." A week went by, and the pain did not stop. On a Saturday night, she went to the ER and after a few hours, an x-ray exam showed some spots that could be cancer.

On the following week, she had the biopsy done and had doctor' appointments already set up. The doctor explained to us what they had found. It was stage-two breast cancer, and she was being sent to Boston Medical Center (we live 20 miles from Boston to have their doctors revise the exams and only they would be able to follow through with proper treatment.

Between surgery and numerous visits to the hospital, and 50 days of traveling back and forth for radiation therapy, seven months went by; all the pills that she needed to take made her weak, emotions and side effects of the radiation that still continues to this day.

It was a hard time for both of us, and I did my best to help her cope with it. She says I did great, but still think that I could have done better. We are still happy together, and life gets better every day.

By going through all of this, I learned some lessons—loving my wife and having her by my side made me understand how blessed I am to have someone who inspires me and supports me (that is another story that I would love to tell you in a future opportunity).

My question to you is this: What do you do when you face difficult times in your life? How do you react?

Many people just start complaining, find good excuses, or enter a state of self-pity. Do you happen to know or have met anyone like that?

The way you show up makes all the difference; your attitude as a powerful being determines the outcomes you make out of any situation.

More than overcoming hard times, it's important how you behave, what thoughts you feed your mind with, and who you have around you.

After going through this hard time, I adopted these principles to my life. I did not have all of them up to that point in life, and they helped me stay on the path to where I came to be today. These principles go along with other intense work that I do, and we all should do if we are to show up with our full potential.

My five principles for a great life:

    Integrity

    Honesty

    Give

    Receive

    Be present

It may not sound to you as good as you may have heard or read in many self-help books—I'm not here to be a helper. My mission in life is to work with people who want to make a significant impact, live a powerful life, and create something larger than him or herself.

Integrity—when I say integrity, I mean someone who does what he/she says they will do. You can make this a habit in your life now if you want to. If you are to meet a friend at 7 a.m., be there at 7 a.m.—don't waste your friend's time. In reality, when you are late, you are stealing their time. The meaning of steal in the dictionary is:

take (another person's property) without permission or legal right and without intending to return it. Especially talking about time, you can never return it to yourself or another. To live a powerful life, you have to do what you said you would do. It not only gives you more confidence, but it also increases people's trust in you and is a way of life of true leaders.

Honesty—implies a refusal to lie, steal, or deceive in any way. The first thing is being honest with yourself. Am I actually living what I say I am? Am I doing the things I want to do or am I lying to myself to appear good to other people or cause good impressions? You can even think honesty and integrity are the same, but they are different. There is no small or big lie—you either are honest or not. The Bible says: **"Whoever can be trusted with very little can also be trusted with much, and whoever is dishonest with very little will also be dishonest with much."**

Give—I think everything you do in life is a seed. If you want to reap good fruits, you have to make sure you have good seed and make sure that you plant it in good ground. If you want to have better financial results, you have to give that seed away; if you want more love, you must give it first; if you want to be trusted, you have to trust; if you want to have more, give more of the thing that you want more. Everyone associates money easier than other things, but this principle works for almost anything in life—give to charity; give to people who need and don't need, so when it is your turn to receive you don't receive just because you need, but mostly because you don't need. If you only give to those who need, your brain will associate that you can only receive when you are in need.

Receive—be open to receive and be grateful to be a receiver. Receiving is a universal law. If you give, you will receive somehow. Many people are good givers, but not good receivers; the best is to become great at both, so you can experience an incredible flow of things and feelings in your life that are priceless.

Be present—being present is one of the greatest gifts in today's world. Have you ever experienced a conversation where you were the talker and the other person was present in body, but far away from being with you and listening? I have, and I was the distant one. The result of that is superficial relationships, poor connections with people, and a life that does not experience fun, love, trust, and all other things in its full potential. To become present is to empty your mind of worries and the future things that you have to do or places you need to be. Live in that moment as the only one that exists; then you can feel, connect, love, and live in full potential.

My experience with my wife has enabled me to live a powerful life and grow in many aspects, although I did not suffer as deeply as she or anyone who is diagnosed with any form of cancer. The word cancer is like a death sentence to those stricken by it. I surely had a hard and yet wonderful process of being by her side and being of help, love, and support. I do understand the hardship of people who went through it with a family member or who are going through this painful process right now and maybe don't even know how to navigate along this journey. What I have to tell these people is that it is hard, but if you allow, it will change your life for the better. Have you ever heard of the saying "everything happens for a reason"? What may be hard is that we do not always know and understand the reasons of pain in life, but all things happen for the glory of God.

What I could only say to my wife was that everything was going to be alright, that she would come out of it stronger, and sure she did. For me, it was tough but alleviating and brought out the best of me in those tough moments. So, today, I can work with people who maybe never had the experience of cancer directly or indirectly, but suffer from other problems that anyone can face in their lifetime.

I'm going to put a few questions for you to pause and ask yourself. Don't just do it for the sake of doing—take a few moments to ponder about them, meditate, and process them carefully. You may have an insight that could change your life forever.

What is it that you want for your life?

If you and I were talking at this moment, what kind of conversation should we have about you that would change your life forever (perhaps a dream, vision, or passion)?

If you were to tell me what makes you strive, what would be at the top?

If the doctors said you only have six months to live, what would you do, what legacy would you like to leave?

Want to go deeper? Stop for a moment, grab a piece of paper, and write down your eulogy; you will love to have been in remembrance for what?

You are reading this great book, *THE CHANGE*. Imagine that three years have gone by since you read *THE CHANGE*. What has changed in your life, what insights did you have three years ago that made a huge difference in your life as you applied it? Tell me what have happened to your life and what have you created in the past three years?

The Stories we tell ourselves.

You probably have already heard or known somewhat about your belief system. Everyone goes about in life and get the results that they believe they deserve. You may even think you deserve more, or you want more, but if deep inside your unconscious mind the belief is not aligned to what you consciously think you deserve or want, it will not manifest in your life.

That is why you should be aware and filter the stories you tell, read, listen to, and or watch on television because they will define the results you get in your life. Do you remember when you were just a kid and the adults that were responsible for you said that you were not allowed to speak or request what you wanted? Or that money is hard to get? Or that you do not deserve this or that because..? Or that you could not achieve that dream because it was too big for the poor and little you?

That was what they believed about themselves and did their best and with love to pass it on to you. They were just protecting you and surely if you do not recognize that it was their belief system and that you can have your own belief or paradigms, they will affect your life in many aspects and perhaps you do not understand why.

Maybe you are successful, or maybe you have achieved a lot in life so far, and I am sure you want more. As Rich Litvin says: ***Precisely, what helped you get to your current level of success is what will hold you back from your next level of success. Or to put it more succinctly—what got you here won't get you there.***

If you want to play a bigger game in life or go to the next level of success you want, you must increase your performance. Or if you are a high performer already, you may have to do some tiny changes in direction or in what you believe that makes you a high achiever so you can go beyond the current level.

Back to the stories you tell yourself. What excuses have you been thinking of or spoken out to the world about you not being able to achieve more or become more? Maybe these are good reasons why you could not get a promotion, start your business, make a difference in the world, and have a vision so powerful that makes you unstoppable.

And when you only have a vision so powerful that makes you cry and makes you overcome the fears that are impeding you from taking actions, that will lead to the results you want, only then will you become unstoppable and do whatever it takes to conquer your dreams and make a big impact in the world. What are the three words? **Whatever it takes.** Becoming a whatever it takes person makes all the difference between dreamers and doers. You have to have big dreams to keep you moving, but you will be unstoppable on the way to make it happen if you do whatever it takes—got that?

Put your hand on your heart and say it out loud.

I am going to do whatever it takes to achieve my dreams.

Your words have power.

That brings me to the continuity of the above. Your words have the power to change the course of your life, to change your current situation—no matter what kind of situation you are living right now, you can change your world by changing your words.

If you keep saying to yourself that it is impossible, that you don't have the money, that you don't know the people, that you live too far, that opportunity is not for you—that is what you will get. The Bible says: ***Faith is the confidence that what we hope for will actually happen; it gives us assurance about things we cannot see. Hebrews 11:1.***

Even if you cannot see any possibility, you must declare what you want as if you already have it; that is faith and faith will manifest at the right time what you hope for. Is that powerful?

From now on, I want you to pay attention to what you say to yourself or others, and be aware that it will manifest the results that you are speaking into your life.

Once again put your hand on your heart and repeat after me:

I watch the words that come out of my mouth and I only say what I want to manifest in my life.

Your word is a law, and it must come to pass, when you live from that place you will achieve more of what you want because you start to think and say great things about yourself and your projects.

A client of mine increased his business revenue by 25 percent in a year from an insight he had during a conversation with me. He applied this in his life and business, started saying and doing things as if they were already true, and it started to manifest in his life/business.

Action takers

Words change the direction of your life only when you decide to take actions that sustain your words. That is what makes a huge difference between people who apply what they learn and those who do not apply and keep blaming others or blaming his/her situation, economy, government, etc. You are responsible for your life's outcome; if you are not yet playing a big game, that's on you. Start doing things as successful people do and notice changes in your life.

Are you coachable?

Are you willing to not only receive instructions, but are you willing to be challenged to do what scares you, dive into your fears and your holdbacks, and dare you to move beyond what you believe is possible for you?

If you already playing a big game and are a leader in business or any other field and are making a big impact in your world or community or perhaps making a difference in many lives through your leadership and other capabilities, you don't need a coach, and because of that, you do want to have a coach. Why? Because you understand that you've come very far in the journey of life and deep inside you crave for some more.

What if I am not a high performer or I haven't achieved much in life?

And I do have a question for you—are you willing to achieve the impossible?

What is impossible for you may not be impossible for someone else. Are you willing to ask bold questions? Are you willing to be bold in your quests? Or will you keep playing small and living a limited life?

Impossible, what is yours?

Do you have a dream that is bigger than yourself? Why are you here on earth? Is there a reason for you to be where you currently are? What do you think needs to happen so you can feel fulfilled?

My invitation is for you to start taking actions in the pursuit of your happiness. And it requires an alignment of your words, body, soul, and spirit. When you operate in synchrony, you will achieve what you want. Your fears will be the bridge from the world you live in to the one you want to create, and creation makes all the difference.

What would you like to create in your life that would make you feel great?

What would make you cry if you achieve it?

What makes you cry or embody a whatever it takes attitude to achieve?

What gift do you have that the world longs for it so bad that you cannot die unless you make it happen?

Create the impossible! You are worth it.

All things are possible.

***

To Contact Jose:

Facebook:

https://www.facebook.com/createtheimpossible.coaching

Website:

createtheimpossible.com

Email: jose.createtheimpossible@gmail.com

Phone: 1508-630-5985

Laura Thompson, ACC, CEC, ELI-MP

Known by many as the "go-to" Certified Executive Coach and Life Empowerment Coach in Manhattan, Laura Thompson's motto is "Lead the Life You Desire." She works with individuals, entrepreneurs, mid-level managers to executives, transforming their challenges into opportunities to thrive in a fast-changing world.

Her coaching expertise revolves around personal and professional development, aspirations, transitions, narrative coaching design, mindful communications through self-awareness and effective listening skills, emotional and social intelligence, goal setting and strategic planning, and people management.

Laura's career started out in finance, then she made a career transition to marketing communications at one of the world's largest communications firms, WPP: Advertising, Branding, Public Relations, and Digital Marketing which gave her the foundation to launch her own Global Media Ventures company, Loralia LLC. Laura has worked across industries from startups to the Fortune 100 in the Americas, Europe, Middle East and Africa, India, and Asia. She earned a Master's degree in International Relations and International Political Economy from Boston University in Paris, France, studied at INSEAD, and is bilingual, speaking both English and French.

The Art of Mindful Communications

By Laura Thompson

The art of mindful communications combines effective listening with awareness of yourself and others. Thich Nhat Hanh, a Vietnamese Zen Master, says that once you learn to commune with yourself, you're better able to communicate with others with empathy and compassion. You can develop all these skills at the same time. Initially, I'll describe three levels of listening: Subjective, Objective, and Intuitive. Examples and practice techniques will be given to illustrate how listening is an active process, not passive. Thereafter, I'll explore connecting and communicating with yourself to understand mindful awareness. These two principles are the foundation of becoming a mindful communicator. After all, don't all of us want a better world to live in, and the opportunity to have more meaningful, loving, and productive relationships, whether it's with our family and friends or collaborating with our colleagues or being of service to our clients? The answer is yes, and…

The first principle building the foundation of becoming a mindful communicator begins with the three levels of effective listening. The first level of listening is characterized by "Subjective Listening" and it's how most people conduct a conversation. It's more about the listener's agenda and how his or her experiences relate back to what the other person is saying. Let's take an example of two female startup entrepreneurs who are hardworking, motivated about building their respective businesses, and supportive of one another. On a very hot, sunny, and humid day in Manhattan with a heat index of 108°F, Claire decides to go to Central Park and calls Margot. Claire says, "I can't work today. I don't know what's the matter with me. My air-conditioning is not working properly, the humidity makes it hard for me to breathe and here I am, sitting on a rock under the shade of the gorgeous trees in Central Park." Margot replies based on how she's handled similar situations in the past. Margot says, "I've learned to let myself take it easy whenever I couldn't concentrate or be productive and found the following day, I was able to accomplish everything I wanted to do and much more. Just take it easy." Although this sounds like good advice from a friend and colleague, Margot related to Claire's problem based on her own, past experiences. There is nothing wrong with subjective listening, but it is based more on the listener's experience versus the needs of the person who initiated the conversation. In this case, Claire might have agreed with the kind advice or felt frustrated because she wasn't seeking a solution since she only needed someone to listen to her woes. Most times, women support one another without advice but will relate similar experiences as a means of sympathizing, whereas men often listen with the intent of coming up with solutions. The key word here is need. What are the needs of the person you are listening to? This takes us to the second level of listening called "Objective Listening."

Objective listening is focused on what the speaker is saying without adding the listener's personal agenda. It's effective because the listener lets the speaker know that he or she has really listened and cares about what is being said, in effect, acknowledging what the speaker has said and validating how the speaker feels. Practicing objective listening, along with acknowledgement and validation, increases the skill of effectively communicating at a higher level. We want to keep increasing our level of listening skills step by step until we become a master at listening, thereby creating the life we want to lead.

Now, we'll take two colleagues working for a large, financial institution and illustrate this second level of objective listening. Sami complains to his colleague Michelle, "I have the world's worst boss. He's a jerk. They should have promoted me rather than hire that guy from the outside. He doesn't have a clue how this division works." Michelle replies, "It's normal to be upset because you felt that you should have been the one promoted." In this case, Michelle demonstrated that she really listened and cared about what Sami said by acknowledging his desire to be promoted and validating his feelings of being upset, but with no judgment. Michelle didn't take sides with Sami, agreeing that the boss is a jerk. Instead, Michelle validated Sami's perception of the situation because she didn't know the boss's point of view. This illustrates how everyone has diverse perspectives in viewing situations because of their different past experiences.

Developing the additional skill of comprehending differing viewpoints enhances communication among people in all areas of their lives. The objective is to effectively communicate so that we have better relationships that are positive in nature, which brings us to the third level of listening, "Intuitive Listening." As we fine-tune our listening skills, this third level is an excellent one to operate from on a consistent basis. It's like listening from a

360-degree perspective. The listener pays attention to the speaker's tone of voice, picks up on his or her energy vibration, his or her body language, his or her feelings, on top of what's being conveyed through the conversation. The listener intuitively connects with the speaker, picking up on the underlying message.

Sometimes, it's about what the speaker is not telling the listener and it's for the listener to act like a detective and uncover the real message. I'll admit this is a skillset that coaches such as myself practice with their clients so that we can find out what's really important to our clients as well as understand who they really are and how that's different from the façade that they portray to the world. This is important because we all want to lead authentic lives. Besides coaches utilizing intuitive listening, this is a valuable skill for everyone to have, in order to establish better communications, achieve win-win scenarios, create amiable relationships, build cooperative communities, and eventually, world peace. Is that dream unattainable? No, steady progress and practice can move all of us towards this multidimensional listening paradigm.

Here's an example of intuitive listening between two friends. Anne says, "I saw my ex-boyfriend on the front page of the Lifestyle section of *The New York Times* with his wife and their newborn baby in our old apartment. I had to go to my psychologist because I was so angry." First, Marie acknowledges the situation and validates Anne's emotions by replying, "I'm so sorry. This must have been really upsetting to you." Then, Marie answers based on a feeling, rather than thinking too much about it, saying, "Maybe this is showing you that you really do want to get married and have children one day."

In this scenario, Marie knew Anne's backstory because of their friendship; however, you don't need to know the person intimately to utilize intuitive listening. It's a matter of being aware and mindfully present with the speaker as though they're the only person in the world that matters to you at that moment without external interruptions, like looking at cellphone messages or taking incoming calls. In this type of exchange, the speaker has the listener's undivided attention. It can take seconds, a couple of minutes, or ten minutes with the result that both of you walk away feeling satisfied rather than frustrated or hurt.

Practice intuitive listening at home with your family, at work with your colleagues, with your clients, and also, while socializing with your friends. Remember to have some fun and not take life too seriously. Over time, you'll notice how your relationships become more loving, productive, and meaningful. Being aware and practicing these three types of listening methods—"subjective," "objective," and "intuitive," with the focus on intuitive listening—improves your effective listening skills.

The second principle centers around connecting and communicating with yourself with deep presence to understand mindful awareness. These two principles create the foundation for the art of mindful communications. The second principle will be illustrated below and is best achieved through three proven techniques: being centered and grounded through breath, meditating, and understanding what has caused suffering in your life. Many people agree that focusing on breath and meditating make them feel more physically connected to their body and aware of their mind while understanding the causes of their own suffering help them respond with empathy and compassion for themselves and others. Developing the skillset of becoming a great communicator through the art of mindful communications is important because we all want more meaningful, loving, and productive relationships.

Beginning with breath, my yoga teacher, Dineen, has us sit, stand, or lie down depending on what suits our physical fitness best. She then has us breathe in, hold the breath for a few seconds, then breathe out, and repeat the process three times, which appears to be the magical number for initiating mindful relaxation. Breathing exercises ground and center us in our bodies as well as create mindful awareness of our physical presence. As we breathe, Dineen asks us to notice where we feel tension and breathe into the tension to release it. Most of us carry tension in our neck and shoulders and lower back.

Every time I breathe deeply into the area holding my stress, that invariably releases it. After these breathing exercises, my body feels physically nourished, grounded, and centered. Depending on your temperament and passion, you can achieve this sensation of feeling centered through dancing, bicycling, swimming, golfing, or whatever physical activity connects you to your body while receiving pleasure. Sports can get you into the zone—that is, a meditative state—and act as a means of healing yourself and connecting with your inner being. Choose what works best for you—whatever makes your life enjoyable.

Once you're grounded and centered physically, the next steps towards learning to communicate with yourself can be done through meditation, writing down your thoughts and emotions in a journal, and discussing with others their own proven models. Personally, I like to meditate and write in my journal on a daily basis because it brings me peace and insight. Since not everyone is a writer, I'll discuss meditation as a means of quieting the endless chatter in your mind, letting go, and witnessing what is said or not said with your inner voice. Eventually, you'll experience peace and unconditional love.

Most of my Buddhist friends, some of them laymen monks, say you can meditate sitting down, walking, or exercising. Meditating can be for one minute, ten minutes, an hour, all day long, or even longer. It's a way of connecting with your inner self and your inner voice, becoming more aware of yourself, learning to love yourself as you are, having compassion for who you are, forgiving yourself—

essentially, self-care. Meditation is a big door opener, helping you to dive deeper into the nuances of your life.

The last element deals with the notion of suffering. Once you've figured out what has caused your suffering, you become empathetic and compassionate towards others who have experienced similar situations; therefore, guiding better communications. We have all suffered in different ways because we are all on our own unique journey in life. One of the ways I suffered in life was losing the love of my life. He abandoned me. I felt depleted and empty of love with none left to give to others, let alone myself, when it happened. I felt like a victim and hit rock bottom until I was able to get back up and take responsibility for my own actions that contributed to the breakup. As the old adage goes, "It takes two to tango."

With that realization, I was able to shift my energy level from being a victim to a higher energy level characterized by mindful awareness. Also, I view my trials and tribulations as learning experiences. I ask myself what is the lesson I'm meant to learn, then I take a deep dive and discover the reason. This particular experience had me dig deep for answers. I centered and grounded myself through breath and exercise, meditated, wrote in my journal as a way to connect to my emotions that helped me to understand and let go, and discussed with friends and colleagues on their proven methods on how to deal with life's curve balls. All of these techniques led to my epiphany that love is boundless. What a powerful learning experience! Because I suffered, I learned that love is boundless. Apparently, this was a big lesson I had to learn in life. As a result, I'm able to unconditionally love without judgment on a much deeper level than ever before and know the source is never ending.

Moreover, I learned forgiveness, how to understand my ex-significant other from his point of view, and develop compassion for his circumstances that triggered the rupture in our relationship. I'm grateful for this powerful learning experience. It often comes from the people closest to us. All my various forms of suffering throughout life have made me more understanding, compassionate, loving, and kind towards myself and others. Although there are many different ways, the three mindful awareness practices that I focused on—centering and grounding through breath, meditation, and understanding the source of our suffering that leads to empathy and compassion for others—can assist us all on our journey through life. Reflect back on your life utilizing these tools. Ask yourself how you can become a better communicator? Decipher what has caused you to suffer?

When you practice these concepts on a daily basis, it carries over to the people around you like a ripple effect. These tips are meant to nudge you onto the path of self-communication, leading to better communications with others based on empathy and compassion. This is a lifelong process. Have patience with yourself and others. Maintain steady progress. There will be inherent bumps along the path, forks in the road, and choices to be made. Once you've connected inwardly, your ability to connect outwardly with the external influences of your world grows. You will be better equipped to manage and overcome difficult conversations and situations as well as explore possibilities to create win-win scenarios.

Remember to breathe, smile, and respect each person you encounter such as the Indians, Nepalese, and many others who use the ancient Sanskrit greeting "Namaste"—roughly translated as "My spirit honors the spirit within you." In essence, honoring another with peace and respect assists in better communications because you become mindfully aware of both yourself and the other. Therefore, you're able to listen and speak by understanding multiple perspectives that lead to resolving conflict, reaching agreements, figuring out solutions, and exploring infinite opportunities.

Communicating mindfully creates a better life for you, your entourage, and the rest of the world. We are the world. Let's use our presence wisely with mindfulness and awareness so that we can continue on in our journey in practicing the art of mindful communications together. Steven R. Covey, author of #1 National Bestseller *The 7 Habits of Highly Effective People,* said, "Change—real change—comes from the inside out." Hence, self-awareness enables you to lead the life you desire and be who you want to be while being mindfully present with those around you, thereby, creating a better world to live in—this is a paradigm to consciously strive for and improve upon over time.

Last but not least as an anecdote, I believe in the art of civility through communications. Start by smiling at the people in your life, your neighbors, strangers walking down the street, your colleagues at work—you get the picture. As I live in Manhattan in a skyscraper, we have a doorman who greets everyone with "Happy Monday" or "Happy, Happy Tuesday" for every day of the week. He's sincere and brings happiness to all the tenants that he encounters. He'll be remembered for his positive upbeat personality. It's not very hard to smile at someone. They just might have needed your smile at that moment to uplift their spirit. Smiles are usually passed on, moving the positive action forward. In short, practicing being positive with yourself and others makes the world around you more pleasant.

In a conversation with people, use these simple skills that don't need explaining: Listen with respect; think before you speak by asking yourself what might be the consequences of what you say; don't interrupt the speaker, that is, let the speaker finish his or her own sentences; don't be distracted with incoming calls or texts on your cell phone; be engaged by asking pertinent questions, showing that you're genuinely paying attention and interested; be yourself as you are appreciated; say a kind word; and be grateful. These practices can vastly improve communicating effectively with civility. Remember we're responsible for what we say to others; it's a reflection of who we are. How do you want to be remembered?

In conclusion, this journey was about learning how to become a mindful communicator. We explored three types of effective listening skills—subjective, objective, and intuitive. We discovered connecting and communicating with oneself to understand mindful awareness through breath, meditation, and suffering. On a lighter note, we advocated for listening, speaking, and behaving with civility. These blended elements comprise the art of mindful communications.

Communicating mindfully enhances the relationships in your life, whether it's with your family, friends, colleagues, clients, social networks, or strangers. It helps you to live the life you desire to lead both personally and professionally. The art of mindful communications starts with you, then radiates outwards like a beam of light basking the global village in warmth, understanding, and love—hopefully, transforming the world into a better one.

Let's set sail on this journey together when you're ready to enhance your life and your circles of influence. The sunrise and the ocean anticipate that you'll skim that smooth, flat stone across the water to create ripple effects, touching the hearts and minds of those around you. What are you waiting for?

***

To Contact Laura:

Coaching Web site: http://www.laurathompsoncoaching.com

Literary Web site: http://www.loralia.com

LinkedIn: http://www.linkedin.com/in/laurathompson888

Twitter: http://www.twitter.com/LORALIA

Lora Lucinda Andersen

Certified Professional Coach

Energy Leadership Master Practitioner

Published Writer

Motivational Speaker

Founder, Bucket List Buddies International

Energy Leadership (ELI/ELI-360 Assessments)

Law of Being

Lora is a Certified Core Energy Coach and Energy Leadership Master Practitioner, and internationally-known Relationship Expert. She serves as an Expert & blogger for YourTango, has been published in several national magazines, and is currently working on her first book, set to publish in Spring 2017. Lora has collaborated with several top coaches and relationship experts including Dr. John Gray (author of *Men are from Mars, Women are from Venus*), and Charles Orlando. She has been featured on national and international radio shows, including BBC International.

As a Life Coach, Lora loves working with positive, professional women and men who are open to change and want to continuously improve their lives. Lora utilizes her education in Psychology, her Energy Leadership training, her life experience, and her psychic intuition when coaching others to conquer their fears, get out of the box, realize their dreams and create authentic lives that they love!!

A Love Note to All Humanity

By Lora Lucinda Andersen

I sat down today and started writing with the intention to share with you how you can manifest the life of your dreams simply by changing your thoughts, words, and actions. I often speak on this subject, so I intended to publish "Change Your Thoughts, Change Your World." And as I started writing, I realized I was doing more than just writing about energy—I was channeling. And then tears streamed down my face and I became overwhelmed. I realized that God wants me to desperately speak with you. So today, I am setting my ego and my plans aside, allowing the source to speak to you through me. The very fact that you are reading THIS, at this very moment, is because it is the perfect, divine time for you to receive this message. This is for you.

Dearest Beloved,

YOU ARE LOVED. YOU ARE CHERISHED. YOU ARE ENOUGH.

YOU ARE SURROUNDED BY LOVE.

EVERYTHING CREATED, I DID FOR YOU WITH LOVE.

You can tap into this love through the source of all creation. You are capable of wonderful, amazing things. You are only limited by your mind. Be open to possibility and embrace change and whatever comes next. LISTEN for me to speak in your life. As you work to raise your consciousness, you will start to notice I am speaking to you every day through others and through your experiences in this world. Experiences that YOU AND I co-created before you were born. These experiences are meant to assist you in your spiritual growth. All that exists in the physical world is only temporary. YOU are part of a bigger, magnificent, extraordinary, perfect plan.

You must be responsible for your thoughts, words, and actions. This is how you occur to others. Have everything you think, do, or say resonate with your heart and soul. As you do this, you will elevate your consciousness and you will begin to see miracles in your life. How you measure success in life is uniquely up to you. In actuality, there is no winning or losing, no success or failure. That is all man-made.

Try your best not to mirror others' negativity. You are only responsible spiritually for your own behavior on earth. You are NOT at the affect of others. Other people are experiencing their own unique spiritual journey, and yours is specific to you. You decide what is good and what is bad in your life. Everything has its purpose. All that you have endured, struggled with, all of your challenges, all of your wins and losses, are part of your perfect divine life plan. There is a lesson to be learned in every stumble, fall, or heartbreak. It is imperative that you learn the lesson so that you can move forward. When you fail to learn the lesson, it will repeat itself over and over again until you make the necessary change. Do not become a victim by allowing something to control your life. By doing so, you would be playing small. I expect BIG things from you.

Your children are not yours. They are mine. Do not attempt to control or manipulate them into a limited way of thinking. They have their own divine path and destiny. Give your children strong roots and then give them wings. You are charged to raise them with love, kindness, and respect, to protect them and keep them from harm. After you raise them, you must set them free. Let them learn their lessons just like you have learned yours. No matter how much you love them, you cannot pay the price for their mistakes in life. When you free up your resistance and give them back to me, your loving God, you are allowing them to grow closer to me.

Do not allow yourself to be a victim to time. You are on the earth for a minuscule amount of time and time is man-made anyway. The sun rises and sets the same for everyone. You must give priority to the people and things that you love. Failing to do so makes you a victim to time and keeps you stagnant in life. You must free yourself from your past. That is a part of the lesson. Your life is a journey of amazing experiences especially for you that you and I co-created. There is no bad experience. There are only lessons. When you live in the past, you are denying the present that I have just given you. Because time means nothing to me, I do not want to see you stuck. I want to see you loving, growing, living, and experiencing every single moment.

DO NOT allow yourself to be controlled by fear or by the manipulation of others. Have it so that fear has no place or say-so in your life. Have fearless faith in me, your divine Creator. Do not judge, control, or manipulate others. By doing so, you keep them from knowing me. Love others unconditionally without attachment. Love yourself just as I love you so that you can allow others freedom to follow their own path and grow spiritually and connect to me as well.

Accept all human beings and creatures. You are all spiritual beings living on an earthly plane. All beings are connected to the divine, the source of all creation. The body without spirit is an empty shell. Where your spirit goes upon death depends upon you. You have a choice to return to me or not. I AM the nucleus of all love, light, and energy. I AM that from which everything is and was created. You limit me with your beliefs. I AM not religion. Religion is man-made and limited to the human experience and meaning making. The truth is beyond all comprehension to human minds, but your soul KNOWS ME. Your soul knows from whence it came and to where it shall return.

How humans choose to live their lives depends upon their connection to me, the divine creator. Other people, like you and those around you, are learning and growing closer to me every day, and literally manifesting the relationships and experiences that their hearts and souls desire. You will notice that others who do not feel connected to me, the source and creator of all things, find life more difficult. Just like you alone are responsible for your successes and failures, your trials and triumphs, so are they. It is not that your life was easier for you. You know all that you have endured and overcome. The difference is mindset. Some people turn away from me and become settled in life, and some even allow fear and anger to control them. You can bring them to me and raise their consciousness just by showing them love. DO NOT JUDGE OTHERS. Their purpose is divine just as yours is divine. Also, do not enable them, as this will interfere with their life plan and their relationship with me. They must learn their own lessons just as you must learn yours. They have chosen their path, just as you have chosen yours.

BE THANKFUL always and GIVE when you are in need. I will supply you with everything you need. The world was perfectly created for all of humanity. It is up to you to manage the earth with love, respect, and kindness. There is enough abundance to go around. When you create abundance, be thankful and share. When you are in need, be thankful and share.

And most important of all: DO EVERYTHING WITH LOVE.

Have love be your intention in ALL THINGS. By showing others love, patience, and kindness, you are reminding their soul of their connection with me. You will attract high conscious people into your life and others already around you will rise up to match your energy level of vibration as you think, speak, and act with love. Those that are not ready to know me and cannot relate to your spiritual growth will seem to magically drop out of your life, without anger or resentment, releasing your spiritual (karmic) attachment.

Loving you until we reconnect,

GOD

***

To Contact Lora:

(740) 804-6881

For Confidential and Confident Coaching, contact Lora at loralucindaandersen@gmail.com or go to her website to book a session.

www.loralucindaandersen.com

www.facebook.com/loralucindaandersen

Maggie M.C. Slider

I am a Certified Law of Attraction Mind, Body, and Soul Coach, Parenting Coach, Personal Trainer, and Expert Author. My articles are published on ezine.com and self growth.com. I am also the Author of the upcoming book *Find Yourself*…..a guide to authentically connect with your inner self. I am excited for the opportunity to be a co-author in this book, *The Change*[12]. My chapter "Realizations" is about how I finally realized my passion and purpose and the reason for all the previous challenges and hurdles in my life. I am now on an incredible journey and want others to realize that they can be too.

My vision is for women to learn to love themselves first, to be comfortable saying 'NO' without guilt, and to release their fears and limiting beliefs. To have them create a loving soul connection, to find their place of peace and freedom, to build a strong body and clear mind, to always come from a place of empowerment. Along with my guidance and support, they will navigate their journey, and be inspired to create and live the life they so desire and deserve.

Realizations

By Maggie M.C. Slider

I cannot share my life story with you as I only have one chapter in which to do so. I can, however, share a part of my journey, which began August 2001. I had given up my 14-year career with Metro Police as a Special Constable-Supervisor to be home and raise my kids. Finally, after many difficult years of trying, the Universe aligned and my husband and I finally became parents, as we welcomed a son and soon later a daughter into our home. We made a mutual decision that I would be a stay-at-home mum, which is what I did. I filled my time by volunteering at the kids' school. I was the Chair of the School Council, accompanied the kids on field trips, organized fun fairs and fund-raising etc. I cared for other people's kids in my home before and after school and had a part-time job a few evenings a week. In 2005, I enrolled part-time at Seneca College in the Social Service Worker program and graduated with Honors in 2008. So as you can see, being a stay-at-home mum was a small part of my life. Unfortunately, I had not been happy for many years. I wore a mask every day. Although not many people would have known this, I had no self-esteem or confidence and as a result, I got involved in as much as I could to keep me busy and avoid problems at home.

Mid-2010, I had left my 18-year marriage—the hardest and bravest thing I have ever done. This meant that my kids were now going to be spending time at their dad's home. I knew this was a consequence of me leaving, but I couldn't handle it. One night during the week was ok, but when it came to the weekend, my husband would have them. I couldn't function. My kids are my life. They are my Why! I had left my marriage to protect them. They were not beaten…..but other situations were not healthy for them. I also knew that the life I was living was not the life I was supposed to be living. I asked myself regularly, 'is this it, is this all there is? Is this what I signed up for when I got married?" I knew it was not; the only person who could do something about it was me! I knew no one else was responsible for my happiness. I felt like I was slowly drowning, like I was of no importance and what I did was never good enough for anyone. I knew deep inside of me that there was something way bigger, waiting to be discovered. However, I felt I didn't deserve it and could never have it; I wasn't good enough. Thankfully, I had gotten a full-time job, working as an Educational Assistant in the community class at a nearby school. I loved the kids and loved the job; however, it bothered me that some of the kids were struggling so much and had little support. Let's face it—some teachers just should not be teaching, just like some people should not be parents. There is also the problem of schools not having enough man-power to deal with kids who require the extra support.

I had suffered depression in my life to the point where I was in bed for days at a time. I took antidepressant pills, but they made me hallucinate. I was a functioning depressed person for a long time. In Sept 2012, I lost my full-time position as an EA and had no idea what I was going to do. I had very little money in my bank account since my husband had control over all of our money during our marriage and we were still working out my 50% from the marriage. I decided to start applying for other jobs, as going back to casual employment with the school board was just not going to cut it. What other jobs could I do and still manage parenting my kids alone? I became so depressed and felt hopeless and actually thought about ending my life. It had become way too much to handle. I even considered what the best way to do it would be. Thank goodness I love my kids as much as I do because; if not for them, I know I would have done it.

At the same time, I knew I had been on a spiritual connection journey for a few years at this point; however, I didn't get it. It felt very weird, I cannot really explain it but it was changing who I was. I was mostly reading books which miraculously appeared at just the right time and many realizations started happening. I was having readings done by a clairvoyant, psychic friend, who had been placed on my path. I now knew without a doubt that the life I was living wasn't right for me and it didn't feel authentic. I was losing friends because my outlook and behavior was changing. I have never been much of a gossiper, but I will admit I have felt envious of other people at times and wished I had what they had, or felt sorry for myself because of the life I had. I knew it was up to me to make changes, but I was so scared, how was I going to do it? Who would help me? I didn't go talk to friends because they became tired of me complaining about how I felt. I cannot say I blame them—misery brings other people down. I had no family around and I just could not see a way out. I got to the point once again of not wanting to get out of bed, every morning was such a challenge. I dragged myself out then, drove in my pajamas to drop the kids at school, came back home, and climbed into bed till it was time to pick them up again. I really hated my life, but I loved my kids!

A couple of months later, December 2012, Boxing Day at 10:15 p.m., two police officers came to my door to inform me that my husband had died. He had been outdoors skating as he often did during winter and collapsed on the ice from a massive heart attack at age 55. I learned according to the coroner that he had previous heart damage.

Talk about shock! How do you tell two amazing kids that their father had just died?

I cried and cried, but my adrenaline kicked in and my body and mind did what it had to do. I notified his family, friends, and co-workers. The next day at the funeral parlor, I was accused by his brother, in the presence of my kids, of causing his death because I broke his heart by leaving the marriage. I was also told by his brother that my 23 years total with him was just a little bit of a marriage. At this point in my life, I had stopped feeling much emotion. I guess protecting myself and the depression was just making me feel numb, which at this time was a good thing. I decided to be the bigger person and do what was right as the mother of the kids. So I let the nasty things go and stood up as his wife and as the mother of his children. After all, we were still married and I still cared about him.

The real grieving process began after the funeral when the visitors had left. It became more real as the kids had to go back to school after winter break. On the morning of January 13th, 2013, I woke up and I felt the way I had for years—low, sad, depressed, uninspired, and discouraged. It would be a day like any other, me not wanting to get out of bed. I would drive the kids to school in my pjs, come home, and go back to bed. Boy was I wrong! That day wasn't like any other day. The books that I had been reading, the clairvoyant readings I had been having, the affirmations I had been saying, and the counselling I had decided to get were all starting to take effect. I cannot really explain, but I felt different on this day. I still did not really want to get out of bed, but this day I did and even got dressed. I got up, picked up a journal, and I wrote, "Enough is enough! I've had enough of this shitty life. Today is the beginning of the rest of my life and it's going to be different from now on." This was the start of many amazing Realizations.

My clairvoyant/psychic friend had been telling me that my purpose is to be helping and teaching people and that I will write a book. She said I would wake up one day and there would be an email, like an email from God, with information about a course which I would decide to sign up for and that's what I would be doing, that I would discover my purpose and passion. That, my friends, is exactly what happened.

Just over three years later, my life is completely different. I'm not yet making a ton of money, I don't have a fancy house and luxury car, but that's not what matters to me. It matters that I get out of bed every morning now with a smile on my face, with eagerness to start the day, and with so much gratitude for even the tiniest things. I now realize that my "story" was not about the pain, frustration, hurt, or fear, but had become my reason for moving forward and making the choice to change my life. I knew that my life could get worse, stay the same, or get better, and only the latter appealed to me at this point. I signed up for Christy Whitman's 'Law of Attraction' Life Coach course, through the Quantum Success Coaching Academy (QSCA). It's an online/live course: one call a week, a group call every other week, assignments, homework, and practice hours for becoming a Life Coach. I have to be honest; at first I thought the instructors were all on something. How could they all be that happy, calm, and at peace, I thought to myself. But after about three classes, I was hooked. I was assigned a coaching buddy and we hit it off right away and quickly became friends. From my calls with her and what I learned from the course, my outlook and beliefs began to change. I realized that there is never the perfect time for us; it's all up to the Universe to arrange the right time. I realized that I had to take responsibility for what had happened to me in my life—this was not easy but necessary, and it wasn't about other people. I realized that change comes from choice, not from chance. That there will always be people who like me and agree with me and those who don't and that's ok. I began to change my beliefs about how I was expected to act or behave, or even how I should dress. I realized that it's my life and I will live it my way, making decisions which I know are right for me and based on how I feel on the inside. I let go of the values which no longer served me and those that were actually other people's values which I had been raised to believe were values I was supposed to adopt.

I learned the importance of truly loving myself first and that my principles like honesty and integrity are principles that I actually want to live by. I notice my self-esteem continues to grow in leaps and bounds as does my confidence. I realize that the only person I can count on is me, and that there are many people who will disappoint because they don't have the same principles. I started really taking a look at me and what I am all about, what and who I want to be. Saving the world is not my responsibility, but if I can help just one person to really change the way they think, connect to their authentic inner self, enhance their life, and live the way they deserve to live, then I've done well. I realize that there are many soul mates out there for each of us and we can manifest them into our lives. I realize that I am not willing to accept someone who doesn't treat me as I deserve, who I am not physically attracted to, who does not have the qualities I am searching for. I realize that my partner will not be perfect, but that I can love him with all my heart unconditionally. I deserve to be loved for me just as I am, to be treated with respect and for the Goddess that I am and nothing less. I have found my happy, but would love to be even happier with a partner.

I have finally come to realize that I have no need to feel guilt or shame. These are feelings which have been stored in my subconscious since childhood. I no longer allow those feelings and emotions to dictate. Women especially have an amazing way of taking what someone says and making a story out of it based on our subconscious, not based on what was said. I know that I must set boundaries and I have the right at any time to say NO! I'm not perfect, I know that and will never be. It's totally about listening, paying attention to my inner self, and not about pleasing others. No one can make you feel any way that you don't wish to feel. No one should be given that much power over you. I have learned what it feels like to be empowered, not to back down if someone doesn't agree with me, and not to apologize for my strong, independent personality. All of the struggles and challenges I have gone through—believe me there are many more than I have disclosed here—have happened for me, not to me. They are the reason I am here doing what I am doing today and the reason I am here writing this chapter. I have learned so much about what I truly deserve: that there is an abundance for all. It's in no way about competition or about what anyone thinks I ought to do with my life.

I am helping people and giving back to my community which brings me joy. I know that when you give, you receive and you are actually rewarded for giving. I have always been a giver, not a very good taker; however, I know it makes other people feel good to give so I am learning and accepting with much gratitude. I am grateful daily for my amazing kids and for all the little things in my life like a hot shower, my soft comfy bed, food in my fridge. I have learned the hard way why it is so important to have positive vibration and energy and allow myself just to be when there is resistance, anger, or frustration. It will be alright if I just allow it and process it. I have also learned that to be successful, it is all part of my journey. It is not about my ego, it is about what is right and what is authentic for me and my greatest self. I'm taking time to eat a healthy diet, to exercise, walk regularly, and to drink more water every day and I find the more I drink the more I want, although my bladder doesn't always agree! I'm also learning that sleep and fatigue are something which have been changing for me. I have had insomnia for years now but still functioned and still had energy, but in the last month or so I have been fatigued and I am actually taking time to nap when I need it. My body is my temple and I am honoring it. I take time to sing and laugh because it nourishes my soul and helps with my vibration.

This is my journey and I am finally loving it. Life is now happening the way it is meant to and I realize it is not about me being in control. I am now creating the life I desire and deserve. It has not been easy to get to this point, but I know everything that happens, it happens for a reason. All of the hardships and challenges which I have overcome have taught me life lessons. All of the people who have crossed my path have done so for a reason and have been there for a purpose, good and bad. I would not be who or where I am today had it not been for them and for the transactions in my life. I am working on my trust issues and really paying attention to the messages and signs from the Universe, they are guiding me in the right direction. I now know my path, passion, and purpose. There is something way bigger than myself, something I could only have dreamed of before. It is still a dream, one that is being realized because there is no going backwards, only forward. I am standing with courage, with strength, with love in my heart and total faith. I will be that future self that I see, teaching, inspiring, motivating, enriching, changing many lives by helping others help themselves connect to their authentic inner selves, face their fears, releasing limiting beliefs and learning to fully love themselves and live their lives to their full potential.

To Contact Maggie:

Cell: 416 577 3755

jemslider@rogers.com

http://findyourselfcoaching.info

maggie@findyourselfcoaching.info

Twitter: https://findyourself@SliderMaggie

Facebook: https://facebook.com/maggie.slider

LinkedIn: http://linkedin.com/in/maggie-slider-b0bb4959

Stefan Ciesielski

Stefan Ciesielski is passionate about adding value to people.

As most Germans, he likes football, sausages, and enjoys a good time with friends outdoors. But Stefan is also recognized as a leadership educator and highly respected executive coach with extensive hands-on management experience.

An Engineer by profession, he discovered that his real strength lies in dealing with people, which brought him success in sales and customer service roles in Germany, Malaysia, and Indonesia.

After he found his life purpose of developing people, he decided to leave the corporate world after 15 years and started his own business. His experience in various leadership positions at multinational companies like Siemens makes him a valuable partner to other leaders.

He is known as a coaching pioneer in Indonesia, mixing typical German traits like discipline and structure with his easy-going and humorous personality. His commitment to learn from the best made him a certified Marshall Goldsmith Coach and part of the John Maxwell Team.

Stefan is currently running his own company *AsiaLeader* with focus on leadership development. He coaches and mentors managers in their transition to become entrepreneurs and is also a regular guest at diverse radio and TV programs.

"Burn the ships!"
A Life Changing Journey

By Stefan Ciesielski

My story is about change. Huge change. A transformation from corporate manager to independent entrepreneur. From salary to profit. From comfort zone to adventure and freedom.

You can read it, like it, be inspired by it, and maybe follow a similar path. That's entirely up to you. But I hope it makes you at least think and reflect. I hope it gives you some ideas that might trigger action. Some people who have heard the story told me that it's almost like a blueprint for making a big transformation in life. Not just concepts and principles, but concrete actions and steps to move forward.

And it all started when I was about to turn forty.

What's so special about that? Well—in early 2008, I was concerned. I would turn forty soon. Half of my life was over. Would it be all downhill from here?

The good news: I had the other half of my life still ahead of me. Another forty years to either continue what I was doing or to design a new life. It's a choice. What would you do?

Taking Inventory

While I write these lines, I sit comfortably in my living room overlooking the impressive skyline of Jakarta, the capital city of Indonesia. It's 2016 and I have achieved what many people can only dream of. But eight years ago, my world looked very different…

I am an electrical engineer. Prior to turning forty, I had spent my professional life in multi-national companies like Siemens, KPNQwest, and Nokia Siemens Network. A lot of things happened during that time. I learned a lot. I traveled and had a chance to live and work outside of Germany in countries like Malaysia and Indonesia. I had good friends, got married, adopted a kid, worked hard, rose in the ranks, made good money, got divorced, worked harder, made more money, had a house with a pool, a car with a driver, a fancy job title, responsibility for half a billion USD per year. Life was good.

But was it really?

That was the question I asked myself when I was about to turn forty. Somehow that birthday was a special moment, at least for me. Time to pause and reflect. Am I on the right path? Am I happy? Am I doing what I love to do? Or do I need to change something?

It was at this time that, unfortunately, my mother got cancer and needed immediate treatment. And I was on the other side of the world. That was the final push I needed to ask my employer for a six-month sabbatical (effectively unpaid leave). Thanks to my boss it was approved and I was determined to use the time as efficiently and effectively as possible.

Sabbatical

Before the sabbatical began, I set two goals for myself: first, to help my mother get through a major operation and, second, to make a decision about what I would do with the other half of my life. I made travel plans for the coming months, packed my things, and went to my hometown of Dortmund, Germany.

It was very clear to me how I could support my mum. But it was not so clear how to approach the second goal. The situation was unique. I didn't know anybody who had been faced with a similar decision. Finally, I was on my own and had to deal with it somehow. But I was committed and convinced that I could make it.

I started by reflecting on my current situation and asked myself fundamental questions like:

- Where am I now in life?

- What have I achieved?
- Am I happy?

The thinking that you apply here helps you to find clarity, and serves as a first indication of how to move forward from there. You need to be brutally honest with yourself.

Interestingly, despite the fact that I had already achieved a lot in my life, I was not totally happy.

Living for a while in the house where I grew up somehow grounded me. I felt detached from my job and my routines. I was able to pause, think, and listen to my heart and gut. And what I heard was not all positive. I felt that I was not really doing what I would love to do. I believed that I had not fully explored and leveraged my potential. Material success alone no longer drove me forward. I felt I could do more.

So I started to ask myself the next set of questions:

- What am I really passionate about?
- What is my purpose in life?
- What are the key values and top priorities in my life?

At that point, it's very valuable to talk to trusted friends or family members. You can share your thoughts, listen to their views, and get new ideas and honest feedback. You might be surprised by what you hear.

Answering those three questions was basically like coaching myself. Nowadays, I ask questions like that to my clients. I know it helps. It can open a new world for you.

I concluded at that time that "freedom" and "independence" were more important values for me than "security" or "career." I discovered that my values had changed over time. Good to know.

I also realized that I was passionate to connect with other people, help them, and make a positive impact on their lives. I am not a technical person; I need to work with people. Somehow I was not surprised by these revelations. But the process helped me to become more aware of the gap between where I was and where I wanted to be.

It's good to remember the always valid advice of the late Jim Rohn: "For things to change for you, you have to change." I knew there was only one conclusion: I had to change. And I wanted to.

I couldn't sleep properly for days. My heart was beating fast. I was on fire!

I called my fiancée in Jakarta and told her about my decision. She was as excited as I was, but also asked me another crucial question: "Change what exactly?" Good question. I needed more details, more clarity. But the first step was done. And I was determined to take the next.

My mum's surgery was a success and, after she was on the way to recovery, I moved to Bali—"Island of the Gods." I used to fly there from Jakarta to enjoy the relaxing, almost spiritual, atmosphere. The perfect environment to reflect deeply.

I stayed in the villa of a friend of mine for two months and found the peace I was looking for. I also had the chance to meet my fiancée there. She fully supported my decisions and plans and gave me additional strength.

It was clear to me at that time that I needed a bit more structure and guidance to get a more specific picture of what my new life should look like. I was determined to use the remaining time of my sabbatical as efficiently as possible. I consulted successful people, studied books, listened to tapes, and pondered the various inputs. Eventually, I came up with a list of the key elements that I needed to consider. It was not only about a new "job," but about designing a whole new lifestyle. Included in my list were not only things that I would love to do, but also other key areas of life, like people I wanted to be surrounded by, the industry I wanted to work in, the services that I could offer, the place I wanted to work from, etc.

But maybe the most important question that I had to ask myself was:

- What am I really good at?

I was convinced that if I could identify the intersection of "what I love to do" and "what I can do best," I would find my 'sweet spot,' my mission.

It's not easy to figure out what you are really good at. You might have some ideas, but when you consider them in detail, you can easily get confused. However, I made my "talent list" and compared it with feedback from people who know me well.

It surfaced that I am good with people, building relationships, listening, presenting, explaining things … and dancing (oooppsss!).

Analyzing all answers, a sweet spot clearly emerged. Ideally I had to do something in the area of education, training, personal development, coaching, or mentoring.

Somehow, I was not surprised. It was not the first time this had crossed my mind. But when you see it coming to light after a long and structured process, it is inspiring.

Sitting in the beautiful rice paddies of Bali often till sunset, I also started visualizing how exactly I could provide those services, and to whom. And I wrote it all down.

Sometimes I wondered what the native Balinese thought about me when they saw this white guy sitting alone in their fields with a laptop on his knees….

As a next step, I wanted to share this with my family and friends back home. Since my mum was still going through a tough time, I decided to spend the last two months of my sabbatical in my hometown in Germany. When I boarded the plane, I did not expect that the hardest part was yet to come.

Tragedy

After about two weeks in my parent's house, I got the kind of phone call that you never wish to get. A friend from Jakarta told me that my fiancée had been killed in a motorbike accident. I was devastated.

Readers who have had a similar experience can imagine what I went through. But at least I can share with you that I decided consciously to convert all the negative energy within me into positive energy that could help me build a new life. Easier said than done. After I returned to Jakarta, met her family again, and went through her things, a dark cloud of sadness hung over my head for weeks. What helped me at that time was the support of good friends and my pet projects of building a villa and a training center in Bali. Positive distractions.

Resignation

My sabbatical has ended and going back to work helped me a bit to get over the tragedy of the previous few weeks. But with my new goals in mind, I soon needed to find the right time to let go. That's not easy when you have worked in the corporate world for more than 15 years.

Before I started the sabbatical, I was leading the company's service department with almost 3,000 people. How could I give that up together with the daily routine, the challenges, the camaraderie, and most of all…the secure income?

I had appropriate compensation for my position and never worried about money. But as soon as I resigned, this would be history. What about my financial obligations? What about my lifestyle?

Maybe this is the point where many people with similar dreams give up and decide to continue their life as it is. Obviously, their motivation to change (I call it "the pull") is not strong enough.

But I was determined and I believed in myself. I knew that I had to stick to my decision, with all the consequences.

Of course I could not be naïve. I needed to learn more about the opportunities in the education industry. What was my potential target market? Who were my competitors? How could I systematically learn how to coach or teach? How could I create meaningful content and training programs? And, and, and…

I spent my evenings and weekends fully focused on collecting answers from all the sources I could imagine. I was on my way to becoming an expert in the personal development industry within a few months.

Fortunately, with all my experience as a senior manager, I quickly discovered that the need for executive development in Indonesia was high. There are many skilled people here, but it's usually difficult to find those who are willing to step up and lead others.

I had found my niche: Developing talented people into good managers, and good managers into great leaders.

If I could combine my extensive corporate experience with an effective way of teaching, I would have a prosperous future.

It all came down now to drafting a business plan and developing a strategy for the next twelve to eighteen months. I realized that if you know your current situation well and if you have a good idea about your goals, then designing a plan on how to achieve them is not rocket science.

With a solid strategy in my pocket and a warm feeling in my gut, I resigned. Thanks to the support of my former employer, the phase-out period went very smoothly.

It was mid-2009 and I felt free and enthusiastic about building a new life.

First steps

Many people congratulated me on my decision and for having the courage to walk away from my old life and start a new one. I remember many of them saying that the hardest part lies behind me and that I could now focus on the activities that I was passionate about. That's what I thought as well. But sometimes it seems we have to feel the pain first before we can appreciate the joy. There was some homework to be done before I could really indulge in the pleasures of my new business.

I started doing two things in parallel: first, I initiated the process of registering a company. Second, I went through professional training to become a certified coach.

Neither process was as straightforward as I thought it would be. Halfway through the coaching training with my mentor in Singapore, I learned that my mother had passed away. Again, sad news that caught me off guard. I stopped my training, booked a ticket for the next flight to Germany, and stayed there for two weeks. When I came back to Jakarta, I tried to deal with the situation by working even harder. I focused on my company registration application, which was a bureaucratic nightmare. But with the help of a notary, my partners, and two banks in Germany, we got the company founded and registered as PT Langkah Maju Sukses (Indonesian for: "A step forward to success"). We chose "AsiaLeader" as our brand name, reflecting our passion to develop great leaders. Honestly it felt good when I saw our logo appear for the first time on envelopes, slides, and marketing material.

Business Success

After I finished my coaching training and got certified by the International Coach Federation, I was thrilled to get my first clients.

Fortunately, I have vast experience in sales and marketing, which helped me to do the right things. Cold calls, networking events, "elevator pitch," sending proposals, and a lot of hard work. I felt like a beginner again, but sure enough, the effort paid off. I found my first coachees and also closed contracts with two corporate clients that ordered training programs for their managers and sales force. I got something invaluable: customer references.

I wrote program-outlines for diverse topics, all related to executive development and leadership. Quality was of paramount importance (keep in mind, I am German). I hired an assistant and my first local trainer, who was also the author of a best-selling inspirational book. We grew our client base rapidly.

The first time I received payment for services, I felt like an Olympic champion. All the hard work, discipline, and courage eventually started to pay off.

Financially, it was a tough time for me. I really had to scale back my lifestyle. No more secure income. Every month a new challenge. And there was no alternative route. No plan B. I had burned all ships and bridges. No turning back. But I believed in myself and my team and I was sure we would make it.

It took us another three years to expand substantially and book a reasonable profit. Our year-to-year growth rate from startup until today has been phenomenal. We have more than 50 loyal corporate clients, amongst them some Fortune 500 companies and government organizations.

Even if there is so much more to share, it's time to conclude my journey from salary to profits.

It has been an amazing experience. My business success spilled over to my private life as well. Besides finishing the villa in Bali, I made friends with wonderful people across Asia, and most importantly, I met an amazing woman in the hotel where I held a seminar for a big bank and fell in love. Coincidence? I want to believe that it was more like a reward for making the right decisions. When this book comes out, we will already be married.

Conclusion

I have summarized the 8 key steps of my life-transformation here in order to help you start your own journey:

1. **Pause.** Take a good time out to reflect (not just a Sunday afternoon).

2. **Be your own coach.** Ask yourself the right questions (you can find them in this chapter). Or hire a coach who does all that for you.
3. **Be courageous but realistic.** Don't lie to yourself (the consequences can be severe).
4. **Involve your inner circle.** Get their feedback and support.
5. **Find your "sweet spot"** (the intersection of "I want" and "I can").
6. **Decide!** Don't procrastinate (it won't get easier).
7. **Develop a solid plan** (especially for your finances).
8. **Focus!** No "Plan B" (burn all ships behind you).

This list is simple, though perhaps not always easy to follow. But this is the 8-digit code to unlocking the vault of a new, exciting life. These steps have served me well, and I hope they will do the same for you. Start now!

***

To Contact Stefan:

Stefan.ciesielski@yahoo.com

Stefan@asia-leader.com

www.asia-leader.com

https://id.linkedin.com/in/stefanciesielski

http://sccoaching.com/coach/sciesielski1

Armin M. Kittl

The "Webinar-Guru" and called the "German Genius"

SHARE AND WIN – LIVE YOUR DREAM

Armin M. Kittl discovered his sensitive perception in 1989. He dreamed that he would be drawn in the TV show "The Price Is Right" and that he would win. What happened? He won the super price in this TV show.

He found out how he can spread his perception and how he can systematically get information "out of the box"!

Armin M. Kittl belongs to the few people around the globe who can manage the different states of consciousness α = alpha, β = beta, δ = delta and θ=theta; this means that he can consciously perceive things that "normal" people can´t perceive and therefore he has an incredible advantage in receiving new information and new knowledge.

He has inspired more than half a million people and companies from more than 100 countries with his "brilliant thinking and working methods" during the last 25 years.

In newspapers and TV shows, he is called the "German Genius".

His vision:

To help as many people as possible to live his dream and to develop their "Genius"—their UniquePower® so that everybody can live a life full of love, freedom, prosperity, happiness, and joy.

Dream Your Life and Live Your Dream

By Armin Kittl

I think the best way will be If I tell you my story and how my dream was the starting point for changing my life and my awareness.

There were three major milestones that I want to share with you—and you can belief or not.

My name is Armin M. Kittl and I was born on 1st of April 1965.

Please apologize If my English is not as perfect as yours. I am not a native English speaker—I am from Germany and will do my best so that you can follow up and understand my story—and that you understand why I want to help as many people as possible to live their dreams.

In 1989, I studied Business Administration and Psychology at the LMU (Ludwigs-Maximilians-University) in Munich.

Milestone 1 – THE DREAM

On 14th of June 1989, the big CHANGE in my life happened. It was a very hot day of more than 30 degrees Celsius and still during the night—it was very hot.

This night changed my life because I had a dream that was totally different from any other dream that I had before. I always had very intensive dreams, especially when I was a child—but this dream was so intensive and so real that I could not believe it.

It was like a real time travel and I saw exactly how I would win the TV show "The Price Is Right". I could even see the clothes and the shoes that I had worn. Can you imagine how scared I was about this dream? This dream was so realistic and so different to anything else I had before. I was really blown away and my mind could not explain it.

My decision was clear. I must visit the show and see what will happen—I had to find out whether it was a chimera or was there something behind it that I could not explain by mind.

I wanted to buy a ticket for the show and I swore to keep my dream secret until I won the show—but what happened? The show was sold out and I couldn't get any ticket. I was very disappointed and wanted to bury my dream.

Have you heard that there are sometimes telepathic connections, especially between mother and son, also between father and daughter? Probably you will say that this is nonsense—I had the same opinion in 1989. But let's continue.

I hadn't told my mother about my "dream," but some days after my dream she told me that she bought some tickets for the TV show "The Price is Right." I couldn't believe it and I thought 'I'll be upset.' My mother and I went to Munich-Grünwald to the show.

On the way to the show, I told my mother about my crazy dream that I would win—but she only complained that I wore old fucking Espandrillos, an old orange surf short and a surf trouser from Ron Jon's shop close to Cape Canaveral. I bought these clothes during my US holiday in 1988 and I liked these clothes so much—and the most important thing—I wore this outfit in my dream.

The show began. The moderator Harald Wijnvord called Kittl to the stage, Mrs. Kittl. My mother became a candidate—not me. On the one hand I was very disappointed; on the other hand happy that my mother became a candidate. But she didn't win anything. So I thought 'game over—my dream was a chimera.' After the show, we went to the canteen of the film studio to have lunch and then we wanted to leave. In the canteen, the miracle continued. We heard that our ticket was valid for two shows—not only for one! But here I want to ask you the following question. What was the probability that I would become a candidate if my mother had already been a candidate in the morning—we have the same name—KITTL. Usually the probability is 0% because if a Mrs. Kittl was candidate in the morning show and a Mr. Kittl was candidate in the afternoon show, most of the people will call it manipulation or deceit. But the impossible happened. I became a candidate and in a kind of trance, I won the "super-prize."

At first I thought it was a fluke—but from this time, on these kind of miracles and this kind of precognition became more and more.

During the last 27 years, I have had many, many, many experiences and found out how brilliant everybody can become—there are no limits.

I found out how you can use the whole potential of the subconscious with your mind—no beliefs will prevent you from the fantastic life that you deserve. In total, I developed 21 techniques to use the whole potential of the subconscious—and everybody can learn it.

The technics are called "Geniales Denken - UniquePower®".

Geniales Denken - UniquePower® is the result of the optimal combination of heart, mind, and intuition and a combination of concentration and relaxation to enhance the perception and use unused connections of the synapses in the brain. Through this combination of left-right in the human brain, new neural pathways are activated that were previously inactive—and areas of the human brain are harnessed which are not used by almost all people. The perception widens—the mind expands. New possibilities of perception, ideas, and perspectives are created—NEW KNOWLEDGE IS BORN.

E.g. some world-record holders in sports are using my techniques. I explored autism, nanotechnology, out-of-body experiences, lucid dreams, telepathy, and in combination with my experiences I developed the Hypercube-Model and the Hyperspace Language. The Hypercube-Model is a model of 4 dimensional reality.

With this knowledge, you will become the creator of your reality. You can imagine—at first I was alone with this knowledge and I thought I was upset or schizophrenic—but more and more miracles happened. Many of you have probably seen the movies *The Secret* or *What The Bleep Do We Know*.

Perhaps you have also heard about Neal Donald Walsch's bestselling book *Conversation With God*. It was Walsch's way to find out how to communicate with God. In contrast to Walsch's "spiritual way" to get knowledge outside the box, the Hyperspace Language and the techniques of Geniales Denken - UniquePower® have a more scientific approach with the newest findings in brain research, nanotechnology, quantum physics, and morphogenetic fields. I found out how I can meet my "Guide" and communicate with him via Hyperspace-Language. He explained everything to me—how I can get new information about the future, how to enter dreams, how to use lucid dreams, and how to go out of body. It seemed that there were no limits—so I made many tests and had incredible experiences.

So if you want to develop your UniquePower® and to become a Genius, I am very happy to teach you. We will also give free webinars about UniquePower® and you can pre-register (free) in our partner-program http://www.webinars-excellence.com/~en/antrag/registration/index.htm

Milestone 2 – THE WAY TO HOLLYWOOD – The Realization Of The Dream

After I made many experiences and created knowledge and possibilities outside the box, I asked my "Guide"—how can I share this knowledge with mankind? He told me "write a book and make a Blockbuster Movie" with one of these four film directors:

1. Steven Spielberg

2. James Cameron

3. Christopher Nolan

4. Roland Emmerich

Problem number 1 was that I had no book and problem number 2 was how to get in contact with one of these four film directors. I went to La Palma to start to write the book and had no plan about the content.

My mind told me that I had to write a science-fiction book with a lot of action, like a mixture of *Terminator*, *The Time Machine*, and something magic because this is the right stuff for a blockbuster movie that the four film directors would prefer.

So I wrote a book called *The Nanorevolution*. Part 1 and 2 were created by my mind, but then something impossible happened. During part 3, I fell asleep and my hand began to write while I was sleeping. I didn´t know what I wrote and when I woke up, I couldn´t believe the content. The book was ready and the content was incredible—but how was I to bring the book to Hollywood to one of these four film directors?

I didn´t know any of the four famous people personally. How would you proceed to get in contact with one of the four film directors?

I will tell you how I did it. At first I wrote in my social media profiles in Facebook, LinkedIn, and Xing that I need to contact one of these four film directors. Can you imagine the reaction in the social media? I created a kind of shit-storm and most people thought that Armin Kittl was a crazy guy from Germany—other people thought that it was a joke. So nobody helped me. Then I had the next idea. If I don´t know one of these four famous film distributors, I must find someone who knows one of these four. So I started the next approach in the social media with asking many people—"do you know someone who can refer me to one of these four film directors?" No results—nobody helped me. My next approach was to find someone that probably knows someone who can connect me to one of these four film directors. Hollywood is in Los Angeles—so I only had to find a very influential person in Los Angeles who probably knew someone that has contacts in Hollywood and to one of these four film directors. So I contacted Dr. Ivan Misner from Los Angeles. He is called the Godfather of Networking and Referral Marketing. "Please refer me to Steven Spielberg, James Cameron, Christopher Nolan, or Roland Emmerich"—no answer. Frankly spoken—would you recommend someone (someone whom you don´t know) to one of your most important contacts? Probably never.

So I had to find a way to increase my credibility in Dr. Ivan Misner's perception. I joined BNI in Germany, trained a chapter two times, and made this chapter the most successful chapter in Germany in three of four categories—but still no help or referral from Ivan. Then I joined his CNP-Program and it opened my eyes to how I had to build up partnerships. His networking system is based on the process sow – pour – reap and he categorized the contacts in the categories visible – credible – profitable. The more profitable the contact is, the higher the value of the contact is. When I became a profitable contact for Ivan, I asked him again whether he (as the "Godfather of Networking") could refer me to one of these four film directors—but he didn't have the contact. I was disappointed, but then the Law of Attraction worked. I let my spirit go and thought that it was still not the right time for the blockbuster movie. But in 2009, a named called Thilo Schneider visited my Seminar Geniales Denken - UniquePower® and was overwhelmed by the incredible knowledge that you can get by learning these techniques and the Hyperspace Language.

Thilo Schneider contacted Hermann Wala. We met us in Munich and I showed him my vision board and my mind map where he could find the blockbuster project and then the magic happened. Hermann Wala was a good friend of Roland Emmerich. Hermann Wala gave my script of *The Nanorevolution* to Roland Emmerich. I got the answer that the film projects are booked full till 2016, but perhaps....

Let´s see what will happen with the Blockbuster project.

I always ask my guide about my next steps and how I can optimize —my networking, my strategies, my partnerships—and the result of the "Way To Hollywood" was another bestseller seminar called **"Certified Sales And Networking Professional – 99 customers within 99 days without selling."** I optimized the kind of networking, created networking metrics, combined Internet-Marketing, Affiliate-Marketing, and Referral-Marketing and created a system that increases visibility, credibility and profitability. If you use this system, you can even create hundreds of customers a day. It is a system that combines the most successful methods of Online-Marketing, Offline-Marketing, and Sales.

Milestone 3 – SHARE AND WIN – LIVE YOUR DREAM – Together Successful

Milestone 3 is probably the most important part of the change. Here we need your help. I am always communicating with my guide and asking how I can create the most value with my skills and how I can optimize what I am creating. I always meet my guide on a bridge. The bridge is the connection between the physical world (our reality) and the spiritual world (the world of our creativity and unlimited potential).

That´s the reason why I saw webinars as an optimal tool to build a bridge between the offline and the online-world. Meanwhile, webinars do have the highest conversion rate in internet marketing and there is no better and cheaper tool to teach as many people as possible.

Further, there is no other tool that can create visibility, credibility, and profitability faster than webinars. In Europe, I was probably the first who saw the great potential of webinars—that was the reason why many gave me the nickname "Webinar-Guru."

Our mission is to inspire people that TOGETHER much more is possible, and that shared happiness and shared knowledge means double happiness and joy.

We believe that we can achieve this goal with the best possible education and sharing knowledge. For this reason, Webinars Excellence®, as part of the system SHARE AND WIN, was created. We help people to live their strengths, to discover their great talents, and to be aware of their unique power within and to live it.

On the one side, everyone has unique talents and skills; and on the other side, all human beings are connected in a certain way. Once people realize that sharing, mutual support, and a lifetime of learning brings the greatest joy and the greatest interest in life, then it will be possible for every human being to become aware that he is the real creator of his life. Every day and every moment in his life.

The trainers, coaches, speakers, sponsors, agencies, friends, distributors, users, and partners give their best and share their knowledge with everyone they know in order to help as many people as possible. They give the necessary space to grow and to discover their personality, to develop their personality, and to become a powerful creator of life to all of their friends, partners, colleagues, etc.

We invite you to become a real partner and to share great knowledge with as many people as possible—it is free and your dreams can become reality.

SHARE AND WIN – LIVE YOUR DREAM - TOGETHER SUCCESSFUL

From 1st of December till 22nd of December 2017, we will organize the biggest Online Event ever—500 speakers from all over the world and you can join for free. Our target is more than 5 million participants during these 21 days and every participant can become a partner of this unique event.

This event and the System SHARE AND WIN should help as many people as possible to become financially free so that they can live a life full of love, freedom, prosperity, happiness, and joy.

Make the world a place worth living in and to help as many people as possible has never been so beneficial and so easy!

You can pre-register for FREE on www.webinars-excellence.com, get your own website of the event with your own subdomain (which you can choose freely), and share your subdomain in the World Wide Web! **The homepage is a present for you—at no cost!**

As a registered partner, you earn between 30% and max. of 80% on all products and services offered by Webinars Excellence®, SHARE AND WIN, and their partners.

You get commission for

- Own sales

- Sales of your partners (your Affiliates)

As a partner you will:

- Help as many people as possible to live a fulfilling and successful life

- Get great earning potential

- Meet the world's best trainers, speakers, seminar leaders, and experts (online and/or offline) to learn from them and exchange knowledge with them

SHARE AND WIN IS A UNIQUE MULTI-PARTNER SYSTEM

If you know great experts with a great vision and mission— please refer them to me to become part of our group of speakers and coaches. At the end, **you will have my personal contact details and it will be a pleasure if you contact me.**

You can hire me as a keynote speaker, consultant, trainer, or coach. We will always find a way to cooperate.

Here you can find my major topics (keynotes, seminars, webinars, trainings)

Languages (German, English)

NEW THINKING AND WORKING METHODS

1. Geniales Denken – UniquePower® - how to discover and to use your whole unconscious potential

2. Personal Development – The Development Of One´s Personality

*3. SHARE AND WIN – TOGETHER SUCCESSFUL - How To Help People To A Successful And Fulfilling Life *

4. The Entrepreneur Of The New Generation

5. The "Kittl-Brenn-Faktor" – How to become the biggest problem solver

6. You Know More Than You Think

7. Superbrainstorming – How To Think Ahead And To Create The Future

8. Think Different - Think Brilliant - Knowledge Outside Of The Box

9. Genius Must Be "Crazy" - How To Get The Most Brilliant Ideas

*10. Why Lateral Thinking Is An Old Hat - Ingenuity And EXCELLENCE Require Metaphysical Thoughts *

*11. Do What YOU Want – But Do It Perfect *

12. Dream Your Life And Live Your Dream

*13. Hyperspace And Hyperspace-Language - New Knowledge Outside Of Rationality *

*14. Discover Your Infinite Creativity - Your Consciousness *

New MARKETING- AND SALES-METHODS

1. The M-System - Multichannel Sales And Multichannel Marketing - How To Connect The Best Of Marketing And Sales In A Unique Way

*2. Networking-Metrics - How To Achieve Twice As Much Turnover In Half The Time *

*3. How To Combine The 15 Most Successful Internet Marketing Systems Optimally With Networks, Marketing, And Sales And Thereby Multiply Your Sales And Profits *

*4. MULTI-PARTNER SYSTEMS - The Fairest And Most Profitable Form Of

WIN-WIN-WIN PARTNERSHIPS*

5. Leverage-Effects In Affiliate-Marketing - How To Multiply Your Revenues In Affiliate Marketing

6. The Future Of Business-Networking

7. How To Create Trends - How To Optimize Your Marketing And Sales With Webinars - The Highest Conversion Rate In Internet Marketing

*9. 99 Kunden Within 99 Days - NO-SELLING

10. MULTI-BLOG SYSTEMS – Become Google Number 1 And Earn Additional Revenue Streams

11. CONTENT - CURATION- How To Generate Up To 40,000 Leads / Month For free And Fully Automatic With External Websites And A System

*12. Multi-Lead-Generation—How To Generate More Than 100,000 Leads/Month With Various Computer Programs And A System Almost Automatically.

13. Guerilla Sales And Guerilla Marketing

Armin M. Kittl is known in the media as one of the brilliant thinkers of our time and is one of the most recommended speakers in German-speaking countries. He is founder of "Geniales Denken - Unique Power®," founder of the CNSP-Professional-Program and founder of Webinars Excellence® - The Leading Coaches Online.

***

To contact Armin:

ak@webinars-excellence.com

EAGS Events Ltd.

Dettendorfer Str. 25, 83075 Bad Feilnbach, Germany

T +49 8064/2047-10

Email: office[at]webinars-excellence.com

Skype: arminkittl

Kelly Brown

If you're looking for a new way of changing your life or to enhance your basic well-being, Kelly Brown will teach you the tools needed to create a life you will love and empower you to be your best self.

She is a national and international Certified Empowerment coach, Hypnotherapist, NLP (Neuro Linguistic Programming) Practitioner, and a Power of Clearing coach in Psychotherapy.

Kelly focuses in on finding the limited negative belief patterns and reprogramming the brain into a state of peace and calm and the tools to bring pure joy and happiness into one's everyday life.

Kelly's Pacific Northwest Practice has expanded to include national and international clients via phone and Skype. She offers a complimentary first session to include a brief introduction and background along with making sure there is a compatibly as well as a sense of connection with her client. Kelly also offers workshops throughout the year in various locations along with her team.

From Fear to The Power of Love

By Kelly Brown

Throughout my entire adult life, it seems people are always saying you need to tell your story, but where to begin—so much has happened to me. I guess the best way to describe where I am today is to start by explaining where I started from that led me to the spiritual God-loving individual I am today. I am by no means a saint. I lived with my boyfriend of almost 6 years, not knowing he was part of a mafia drug family. The moment I found out, my heart sank; meeting the FBI at my doorstep, my family and I were in shock! to be told "I'm sorry Miss, you are to enter into our witness protection program we have set up for you and your boyfriend. You must say goodbye now to your family forever." My mother and father were still married, never divorced, and my sister was a very young age to leave.

I was scared, frightened, never understanding how a family I loved so dearly never shared who they truly were with me. Since I didn't know anything about the drug trade, or the family involvement, the FBI needed me to sign a legal form stating I would never see my Love again. Not to mention I was never allowed to share with him that I found out the family secret he had been protecting me from all those years. The FBI sat me down and explained how my Loved one's life was in danger, and to be accepting of the fact that he too was dangerous; not to me, but any connection to him would be far too dangerous to bear and there was no way they saw me staying safe… I asked at that moment if there was a hit out on my boyfriend. They in turn said yes, I'm afraid so; he is not going to live a long life if he doesn't choose to cooperate and 99% of the time when family is involved, they do not choose witness protection."

From that moment on, after I signed and agreed to a lifetime restraining order from him and his

Family, my life suddenly went into fear. I lived in constant fear... I could not shake it! I had this dark hidden secret I was not allowed to share with a single soul for the next 10 years of my life. It ate at me every day he went missing. Years went by and I would receive something attached to a bag, a stamp, something only my Loved one and I had a special connection over.

I started having strangers come up to me in the streets telling me my Loved one was safe with God up in heaven—they even said his name to me. They would ask if they could give me a hug from him passed to me.

I agreed; year after year, over and over in different states where no one even knew me, strangers would say your Love is so proud of you, you must not be scared anymore, you are safe. He's in Heaven watching over you always and loves you and just wants to give you a hug... I would ask these strangers to describe him to me. They would begin with telling me his height, eye color, his favorite outfit he always had on, the way his hair was styled, and his bright blue baby eyes always... He just kept saying "I want Kelly to feel safe and live in Love, not Fear."

He Changed me. I started learning about everything having to do with Love and Fear and how we truly can only live from these two places in life.

I looked into hypnotherapy to learn how to calm my mind from fear and the unknown. I was in multiple car accidents while in my relationship with my Love, not knowing the underlying reasoning behind the car ring that he too was a part of unwillingly. I lost a lot of memories of my childhood and every time I had a hypnotherapy session, I would regain one about my grandma or aunt that had passed away, my sister who had died. The memories were beautiful and I wanted more of them and could not continue paying $100s of dollars weekly to piece my life back together, so I became a hypnotherapist myself.

That led me to a love of the brain and all its amazing components and special golden nuggets that lay far underneath our subconscious barriers. I think of it as going in and mining for gold. So special and so unique and rare to find and so tiny are our own memories (golden nuggets), the ones we have long forgotten about.

From there I met so many incredible people who have the same love and passion for knowledge as I do uncovering what our minds are made of. NLP (Neuro Linguistic Programming) became my next passion. OMG I loved it! So simple and to the point to reset and rewire negative belief patterns into something so positive and uplifting. It's like boot camp for the brain and you can recreate all fears you have had in your life. Just like hypnotherapy, you can take an incident that was devastatingly awful and freeze the photo of it in your mind, shrink it, pixilate it, set it on fire, or tear it up. Whatever your mind chooses to do to deactivate the negative electrical impulse you get that's chemically charged to your neuro pathways to desensitize from the fear itself. You will still have that memory but no longer have the negative emotional connection to it. This I love to do with all my clients. It helps them to relive their past, but no longer live in fear.

I teach them how to send that younger self Love, their inner child…
I

fell into Loving, Love. It's my number 1 passion in life. LOVE that amazing feeling loving a flower, an animal, a best friend, your child, your family, all the way down to the cup of coffee you start with every day. The Power of Clearing Coaching I do is a form of Psychotherapy that teaches us the powers of loving our inner child— we all have one in us. That little boy or little girl that so desperately wanted the Cabbage Patch Doll for Christmas that Santa never brought but did for Suzy down the street, or Danny's little Red Rider gun that broke in half and never got fixed like promised. Things that emotionally stick with us throughout our life that we allow to define us in our later years within our subconscious mind.

I'm able to talk through a process that in turns asks the questions that once again pulls up those special golden nuggets hidden deep in our memory bank that my clients need in order to forgive, release, and set free memories that were forgotten and unresolved and never healed from. I work with the Ego and teach how to stay cognitively aware of it when it's active and when we are in our true authentic state of being… which brings us to living in a state of non-ego and LOVE…

It was two years ago my best friend was dying of cancer and I had to stay strong around her to be her support system.

We were flown in a private jet with a couple from the Fred Hutchingtons Cancer research team to Texas to meet with Doctors and the whole cancer team that originally was set up for Steve Jobs before he passed away to fight his cancer. Only to be told by 6 doctors it's too late. Your best friend is going to die. We flew back hopeless, and I started driving hours every day to see my friend with very little sleep, mind you. I ended up in the hospital exhausted, an emotional mess, trying to juggle being a single mom, running my own business and no sleep, being her caregiver every chance I got.

I woke up the next day in the ICU being yelled at—"lay down or you're going to give yourself another stroke!" I thought to myself this can't really be happening; there's no way. I had a stroke sure enough …I'm telling my hand to move and nothing will budge on my right side, yet my eye sight was so blurred all I could see was colors pixilated—even the air was pixilated, my skin, my sheets. I tried to ask what's going on and only a few words could come out of my mouth, then NOTHING! I was scared to death. I was 100% cognitive in my brain, but could not say only a few words. Fast forward 3 months, still can only say a few words, then the word umm umm umm would come out as if my brain was on pause button.

I couldn't believe what my life had become. I couldn't read, write, or think for long periods of time. I was so blessed to have Swissbionic PEMF (Pulse Electro Magnetic Frequency) come into my life along with the Brain wave entrainment device. This PEMF mat came into my life from heaven above, I swear on it.

Within 3 months, I was talking and cognitively functioning the normal way again, the binaural beats helped restore new neuro pathways in my brain where the brain synapses had fried, not allowing my words to flow. Well guess what? Not only do I fully speak, I am now a Public Speaker for Swiss Bionic PEMF Mat and I have also become a rep as well to sell to all my clients and their friends. How many people do you know who suffer with debilitating disease FIBROMYALGIA, MS, PARKINSONS, CANCER, ARTHRITIS, ENDOMETRIOSIS… and just preventative care? Fibromyalgia in other foreign countries is called Pulse Electro Magnetic Frequency Deficiency. Something here in the US that the medical community do not like to talk about.

This PEMF MAT just became FDA approved and even was used in the Olympics… I swear it

saved my life from living with a stroke. My doctor told me it would take around 11 years to get back to my fully functioning self—I showed them. I also used KANGEN purified water with a PH of 9.5. Out typical water is under the right amount of PH and is full of extra added elements that create even more acidity in our bodies—this alkalized my body and mind. I love my life now; I live in health and harmony.

I live in the place of LOVE… I owe it all to my Love who taught me the real meaning of Love. He took his life to protect the ones he loved, especially me, and now I teach Love to Everyone who crosses my path in life. I hope to be crossing your path soon.

To Contact Kelly:

http://facebook.com/kellybrown35

kelly@rightoncourse4u.com

www.RightOnCourse4u.com

Rightoncourse4u@gmail.com

www.RightOnCourse.SwissBionic.com

Phil Bush

Phil has handled a wide variety of assignments in the areas of Sales, Sales Management, Business Development, Channels, & Strategic Alliances. He has worked with the biggest of the big, including Oracle & IBM.

Phil is focused on Sales Enablement. All areas of the Sales Process, including Sales Process Definition, Territory Planning, Account Execution Planning™, Sales Coaching, Sales Team Coordination, & Partner Execution. He has worked with a variety of Start-Up organizations through Georgia Tech's Advanced Technology Development Center (ATDC). He is always Focused on the big picture of Sales Performance to improve revenue attainment.

Phil served as Principal for Atlanta-based Infomentis—now part of Altify—focusing on expanding revenue streams for its clients in all areas. The Client List included Oracle, Microsoft, CA, Cognos, Informatica, & NetApp. In his 6 years, Bush started & developed the Sales Performance Coaching practice, helping client's Sales Teams Better Execute. Phil went around the World in helping sales teams improve their sales success, by as much as 50% in just under a year.

Throughout his career, Bush has devised multiple Sales & Marketing processes with a focus on Execution Success: Sales Methodologies, Repeatable Process, and Consistency of Delivery.

Selling Begins at the Intersection of Urgency and Importance
The Change in Your Sales Approach

By Phil Bush

What we focus on here is to change the matter in which you go about working A Sales Opportunity from Beginning to End. It is not about "Working Harder." It is about Working Differently. The Approach here focuses on specific and tangible ways you can go about Changing how you approach Each Opportunity. For each type of Opportunity—be it Intuitive Demand or Forced Demand—there are specific Steps you need to take.

There are those that would simply say "Selling is selling." Nothing could be further from the truth. In this day and age, Selling is vastly more complex than it used to be. Why?

We live in the Era of the Educated Buyer. Per Gartner, Buyers do 70+% of their Research online prior to even engaging with a Sales Resource. As such, whether a Buyer knows your product or service or just thinks they know, you cannot tell them they are wrong. You must understand that you cannot say "You don't know my Product/Service." That is Akin to calling someone's Baby ugly, which is a bad idea. The Educated Buyer may or may not know your Product or Service. But since they Think they do, that is where you start from!

So, no matter what you sell, be it Product or Service, selling begins at the Intersection of Urgency and Importance. The Flow is always similar. It starts with the understanding of the situation. There are 2 distinct different times of Demand:

- Intuitive Demand: The Buyer Decides they need a Product or Service, and approaches Suppliers for that Service

- Forced Demand: The Seller Decides that a company is a candidate for the product or Service that they Sell

Each requires a different approach. They are not the same, and in some cases, not close to the same. Let's look at each one independently. There are elements that are the same.

Intuitive Demand

The Buyer decides that they have a need for a Product or Service you provide. At some point, they contact you to learn more about the Product or Service. From this point, the Process works about like this:

- Buyer: Indicates they want to learn about the Service/Product that the Buyer Offers and contacts the Seller
- Seller: Responds to Buyer. This is where the Sales Process begins. Sellers who are contacted must understand what they are going say to the buyer. There are 2 distinct Skill Sets at Play:
    - Strategic Questioning: Focusing on the 3 Layers of Questions that define a Real Opportunity
    - Strategic Listening. A focus on not Listening to Hear but Listening to Understand. It is a very Different type of Listening. You must figure out the best way to go learning and translate the Buyer's questions into what you can do next.
    - Understanding the Intersection of Importance and Urgency and how it impacts the Buyer
- There are 3 levels of Questioning in this situation:
    - Why is there a need:
        - How is it being done today?
        - What is missing from how it is done today?
        - Why Now, Why Not Last Year?
        - Why Not Next Year?
        - Who is indicating it is a Priority?

In sales, I do not believe in Coincidences. Things happen for a reason. What are the possible answers to the Why Question:

- A new person has come in and it was a Key Priority for that person.
- A new Division of the company has demanded the they get a Product or Service that looks like what you offer.
- The current method of doing it is out of date or no longer works.
- A Process Change has resulted in the need to change the Product or service that supported it.
- Is the Buyer the buyer? What Role does he have in the process? Most Sales situations start out with a person who is not the buyer making initial calls to learn and then others may get engaged.

Upon understanding some of these answers, it leads us to another aspect of things that need to take place. The "Who" questions. The Who questions help you understand what needs to be done by the Buyer's company.

Next, we look at the nature of the Who:

- Who is the Buyer, really? The person who contacted you may just be the first person you must talk with. THEN, the real evaluation begins. The Buyer may be Assigned to look at the Products or Solution, but themselves could not buy anything!
- Who is making the decision? Is it a person, is it a committee, who is it?
- Who is Signing the agreement to buy what you Sell? Do you know? Are there multiple people to sign off on this Buy? Do you know who they are? Have they been revealed to you? If not, you don't have a real opportunity if your Prospect will not reveal this.
- How will they go about using your Product or Service? Have they decided? DO they have a plan? Are they counting on your help to make things work correctly?

So, the Who part then takes us to the actual Core of the Buy. It is the nature of Urgency and Importance.

The nature of Demand is that we cannot spend all our time overthinking this situation, but we can learn, as a summary:

Is the Need Urgent and Important, and if so, is it to the same person? If not, there is a chance that you get caught in one of these situations:

- **Urgent, but Not Important** – This is called "Important to Who?" or "Do we have to?" It may be Important to certain entities, but it is important to understand that it is both Important AND Urgent and to people or groups that matter. If not, then you can spend a lot time working on a need that, While Urgent to some, is not Both Urgent AND Important!
- **Important, but Not Urgent** – This is called "Not Now." While it may be Important to some, it will not happen just now, as it is not as high a priority as other items that need more immediate attention. Or, it is Important to some, but the same people who do believe in its importance, but will not elevate it to a higher level ahead of other things.
- **Not Important, Not Urgent** – This is referred to as a "Science Project." Someone will be assigned to look at things, but will not be authorized to DO anything. So, a Science Project Looks like a Real evaluation, but is not Going to result in a Purchase. This is where you as potential Supplier can spend a lot of time. So, be Wary of Science Projects. They will eat up your time, but not result in anything happening.
- **Urgent AND Important** – This is where Real Business Happens. As a Seller, you should Prioritize your time to where 90% should be spent on Evaluations that are Both Urgent and

Important. If you can validate this as a Seller, you will be much more successful.

If you get to where you can confirm that it is both Urgent and Important, you have a real Opportunity. Now, read the information on "Timeline to Go Live – Joint Execution Plan" to understand a Change in your process that will take you all the way to getting this done.

Forced Demand – Seller Created

The Buyer had no interest in your product or service until you put the idea there.

- Buyer: Indicates they are willing to learn about the Service/Product that the Buyer Offers
- Seller: Responds to Buyer. This is where the Sales Process begins. Sellers who are creating demand must be even more careful in what they are going to say to the buyer. There are 2 distinct Skill Sets at Play:
    - Strategic Questioning: Focusing on the 3 Layers of Questions that define a Real Opportunity – Particularly important when the entire process Started with the Seller. The Buyer should earn each moment of time!
    - Strategic Listening. A focus on not Listening to Hear but Listening to Understand. It is a very Different type of Listening. You must figure out the best way to go about learning and translate the Buyer's questions into what you can do next. What about your offering got them to take the time to talk with you in the first place?
    - Understanding the Intersection of Importance and Urgency and how it impacts the Buyer
- There are 3 levels of Questioning in every situation:
    - Since the Buyer was not interested, what has got them interested in at least having a conversation about your Product or Service:
        - How is it being done today?

- What is missing from how it is done today?
- Why Now, Why Not Last Year?
- Why Not Next Year?
- Who is indicating it is a Priority?

If you got this far by just getting a conversation started, then you should look for Why they took your call in the First place. Things happen for a reason. What are the possible answers to the Why Question?

- A new person has come in and it was a Key Priority for that person.
- A new Division of the company has demanded that they get a Product or Service that looks like what you offer.
- The current method of doing it is out of date or no longer works.
- A Process Change has resulted in the need to change the Product or service that supported it.
- Is the Buyer the buyer? What Role does he have in the process? Most Sales situations start out with a person who is not the buyer making initial calls to learn and then others may get engaged.

Upon understanding some of these answers it leads us to another aspect of things that need to take place. The "Who" questions. The Who questions help you understand what needs to be done by the Buyer's company.

Next, we look at the nature of the Who:

- Who is the Buyer, really? The person who contacted you may just be the first person you must talk with. THEN, the real evaluation begins. The Buyer may be Assigned to look at the Products or Solution, but themselves could not buy anything!
- Who is making the decision? Is it a person, is it a committee, who is it?
- Who is Signing the agreement to buy what you Sell? Do you know? Are there multiple people to sign off on this

Buy? Do you know who they are? Have they been revealed to you? If not, you don't have a real opportunity if your Prospect will not reveal this.
- How will they go about using your Product or Service? Have they decided? DO they have a plan? Are they counting on your help to make things work correctly?

So, the Who part then takes us to the actual Core of the Buy. It is the nature of Urgency and Importance.

The nature of Demand is that we cannot spend all our time overthinking this situation, but we can learn, as a summary: Is the Need Urgent and Important, and if so, is it to the same person? If not, there is a chance that you get caught in one of these situations. Why were they not looking before? What Nuance of what you said got them to further Engage? It is important to find out the key things about what you want to have happen. Is the Demand:

- **Urgent, but Not Important** – This is called "Important to Who?" or "Do we have to?" It may be Important to certain entities, but it is important to understand that it is both Important AND Urgent to people or groups that matter. If not, then you can spend a lot time working on a need that, While Urgent to some, is not Both Urgent AND Important!
- **Important, but Not Urgent** – This is called "Not Now." While it may be Important to some, it will not happen just now, as it is not as high a priority as other items that need more immediate attention. Or, it is Important to some, but the same people who do believe in its importance, but will not elevate it to a higher level ahead of other things.
- **Not Important, Not Urgent** – This is referred to as a "Science Project." Someone will be assigned to look at things, but will not be authorized to DO anything. So, a Science Project Looks like a Real evaluation, but is not Going to result in a

Purchase. This is where you as potential Supplier can spend a lot of time. So, be Wary of Science Projects. They will eat up your time, but not result in anything happening.
- **Urgent AND Important** – This is where Real Business Happens. As a Seller, you should Prioritize your time to where 90% should be spent on Evaluations that are Both Urgent and Important. If you can validate this as a Seller, you will be much more successful.

If you get to where you can confirm that it is both Urgent and Important, you have a real Opportunity. Now, read the information on "Timeline To Go Live – Joint Execution Plan" to understand a Change in your process that will take you all the way to getting this done.

Timeline To Go Live - Joint Execution Plan

Coming out of this, the key is to have a Joint plan around How you get from an Evaluation phase to having something done. The Traditional way for this to happen is a Close Plan. The Problem is that a Close Plan is a One-Way Document. It is all the things the Seller should do to get the deal.

What if we changed the Dynamic? Picture this conversation with a Prospect who has expressed Interest in your Product, and they are giving you positive Feedback:

> Seller: "So if you decide that you like our Product, what has to happen for you to move Forward with our Company and Acquire the Product/Service?"

> Buyer: "Well, there are a variety of approvals we have to get, and there may be some Executives who need to sign off."

> Seller: "Can we lay out all of the Buying and Selling Steps together? That would make sure that I was putting the right Resources that will ensure you get your Evaluation Done. It

also puts down in Writing Not only what you need to buy the Product, but taking you all the way to when the Product is Live at your company. Does that make Sense?"

If the Buyer says no at that point, there are a few reasons why:

1. Buyer says it is too Early in the Process to do this.
2. Buyer says they don't know.
3. Buyer says "It is all on me. I will figure it out."

Any of three are Problems, why:

1. It may be too early, but you want to know Early in the process to take appropriate actions.
2. The Buyer not knowing, but being willing to find out, tells us that they are serious and interested. But Not Knowing is not a great thing, and it may show us that the Transaction is not well thought out yet.
3. Rarely does Buying Anything of substance not involve going through Many steps, unless you are dealing with a very small company. If you are dealing with a Senior Executive, that is fine, but otherwise it is Seller Beware; most often these situations involve a lot of time spent by you, and no assurance that Anything will happen at the end of the Evaluation

The Joint Execution Plan is done with the Customer, and include Buying and Selling Steps, intermixed into one document. It includes all the Selling Steps and Buying Steps, then Continues till the product is up live and Operational.

This tells the Buyer you are very concerned not about just "Selling" something, but in Ensuring that the Buyer Gets Real Value for their product.

A Summary

Real Business happens when one understands the nature of Importance and Urgency for addressing each item regarding the

Service or Product you Sell. It is a Combination of Who that indicates they are achieving something Urgent and Important with the Classic Notion of Why and Why Now.

- Why is Important?
- Why is it Urgent?
- Who is it Important/Urgent To?
- Why is it Important/Urgent Now?

Every Item you are working on as a Seller should include a listing of these 4 Items. IF you cannot answer every question—not for your Boss, but for yourself, you must ask yourself if you have a deal that is real?

Each of these items are not by themselves unique. Sellers hear them all the time. What I hope you take from this is the Intersection of these elements, if asked Correctly, will give you a real sense of the "Reality" of the situation you are attempting to address.

Also, answering the WHO questions will allow you to focus your selling efforts on the right person within the customer organization.

This will help you Know that you have or don't have a Real Sales Situation.

Don't just Start Selling and hope that you can Create a Deal. You can spend your time much more effectively by Working "Real" Demand. You can Force the Demand by asking the right questions, but you should Qualify things very completely.

Too many sellers start Cycles without understanding the Nature of the Demand. Where it came from, what prompted it, and what caused them to look at what you must offer in the first place.

If you Spend More than a Cursory level of time and Do Not Understand the Intersection of Urgency and Importance, you are likely Wasting time and don't even know it.

psbush@bellsouth.net

4048404927

Radio Show/Podcast: https://goo.gl/clwszs

Blog: www.dailysalesthoughts.com

Yves Deceuninck

Yves started his career as a French teacher in a high school in Canada.

Twenty-five years of experience in banking around the world, including Europe, Africa, Asia, Bermuda, Guernsey.

Active in the Microfinance sector (Africa, Eurasia, Eastern Europe) guiding and coaching board members, CEOs, and risk managers on risk management, internal control, and governance.

Has obtained Master's degrees in Applied Economics, Financial Risk Management, IT Network and Organization, Internal Audit, International Finance.

Provides training and seminars in Central banks around the world in the fields of Finance.

Certified ICF coach, he is focused on performance coaching and emotional performance to achieve personal, sport, and business based goals.

He also studied Sports Psychology Performance Coaching with Dr. Joann Dhalkoetter, coach of US gold medalists, and Somatic Coaching with Joesette Lepine, former dancer at Opera de Paris and followed a bachelor in psychology at University Paris.

He developed cohesive performance programs for teams and individuals combining mind, body, and emotions. Performed research on mental resilience for special forces units and is in the process of obtaining Anti-terrorism Fight qualifications

Sports-activities: boxing, self-defense, walking, meditation

Impressed by ordinary people doing non-ordinary activities; like my mother, Vincenzina Panaccione, giving more than 25 years of her life as a volunteer to help the poor.

A Whiter Shade of Change

By Yves Deceuninck

In the world, and specifically in the business world, we talk a lot about changes; every day we see in the press, on the internet or television, a debate on delocalization, a restructuration, new tech products, new CEOs, new regulations or market volatility.

It seems that everything is changing except our day-to-day life. On and on, over many years, we repeat the same patterns; we have the same reaction to specific situations. We generally live in our comfort zone and we do not change.

When you ask your neighbor or colleagues how their weekend was, we usually receive the same answer—nothing special, the usual routine; in other words, we are always using the same brain connections and the environment has the power over us. We are the spectators of our lives, and our boss, wife, husband, and children dictate what we have to do. We promise ourselves that once the kids are at university, and if we get a nice boss, we will be able to think about our inner needs. But in the meantime, we experience other constraints and postpone our ambitions.

A young French philosopher, Etienne de La Boesie, born in 1530, wrote an essay at the age of 19 (or 22 for others, a big debate in itself!) named "Discourse on Voluntary Servitude." The assertion of de La Boesie's essay is that we give up our freedom to the tyrant, society, the elite,…let us say to the surrounding environment.

Above the fear, it seems more comfortable to accept the status of courtesan where one can scrounge a bit of power from the hierarchy in place.

Nowadays, we continue to debate about the subject of servitude, evidence that with all the changes the human world faces, new technology, massive improvement in medical treatment etc. the fundamentals of the human attitude, behavior, and questioning remains the same. In the market of coaching and personal development seminars, the availability of non-violent communication and other "be yourself" programs are flourishing. People realize that they can change and are ready to change and by the time they go home after the seminar, the majority of them forget to apply the principles learned and revert back to their old ways, what they used to do and experience before, and we are back to square one.

Without really knowing why, we obey rulers, we have an option of withdrawing without violence this obedience to the rulers and live our core values. From that point, we can co-create with our surrounding environment to make a better world for us. A world where we decide to exist without rejecting others. Many will agree with this statement, but it is here that the social psychologists will opine that human beings are gregarious animals and being part of a group is fundamental to their existence. Many human beings believe that remaining in a group and thinking like the group is easier because they feel that the social cost to exit is too high. You have to choose being yourself or being them; and in some cultures, this statement is even more difficult to live by as you are totally rejected by the community. Being you or being an avatar of you created by others. Are you not more than an image, are you not more than the perception that others have of you after meeting you for 10 minutes. Are these 10 minutes more important than what you have experienced during 20, 30 years, or even more.

By the way are we in 2016 or 1530, is de La Boesie our contemporary?

We all think we are logical, we are taking rational decisions; however, we have to admit that we are subjective. Research in cognitive psychology shows that we are less rationale than we think, biases are affecting our decision making. Psychological biases are the tendency to deviate from a standard rationality. There are many biases, we give a few examples:

•the status quo bias is the tendency to like things to stay relatively the same (to remain in your comfort zone),

•the information bias is the tendency to seek for information even if it will not affect action (this delays action).

Another example is the framing effect (Tversky & Kahneman): human beings have the tendency to avoid risk when a positive frame is presented and take risks when a negative frame is presented.

All our decisions are dependent of a human characteristic, our emotions. Our emotions play an important role in our decision process. The slogan could be: Change your emotions and you will change your decisions and change your decisions and you will change people's emotions. Change your emotions and you will change and the world will change.

Paul Ekman, the famous psychologist, identified seven emotions that have universal signals: fear, sadness, anger, contempt, disgust, surprise, and happiness.

As we can see, many are negative emotions. The polarity of the emotions you feel will affect your decisions. Suppose that on Monday morning you are in a bad mood and you feel anger, it is very probable that if you have to take a decision, your perception of the problem will be negatively biased as well as your decision. Imagine the same problem with another emotion, let us take happiness, it is very probable that the decision taken will vary from the one with your negative emotion because our emotional state gives us a different vision of the reality. Decisions are affected by our limbic system (emotional brain).

Don't make a decision when you are in a peak of negative emotions. Postpone it, but "impossible" you will reply, "I will lose my credibility," so difficult to change, isn't it? That is the power of our beliefs. The weakness of the so-called strong people.

We have to admit that we are subjective and our emotional state plays a major role in our vision of the world, our decision, our actions, our relationships with colleagues, friends, family, and other people.

Last month I attended a seminar on the topic: what is your relationship with money. During group exercises, I noticed a number of participants blaming their parents for all the difficulties they faced during their life. If they failed, it is because of their parents not them, they were victims. When does it stop if their parents explain that it is because of their parents and finally it is because of the Neanderthals. The so-called "black sheep effect."

We are clearly here in a blaming situation that can be synthetized by the Karpman triangle where we have a victim, a rescuer, and a persecutor, all the actors of a conflict in fact. During the training, the victims were the participants, the rescuer was the trainer-coach, and the persecutor not present, the parents. By using and keeping this configuration, a trainer could create a dependency and keep the power on the participants. Although an action can be perceived as a desire to change, it actually creates a status quo or even worse a reinforcement in the status of victim and the need to have a rescuer on a permanent basis. You will feel better for 5 minutes after the seminar, then like a drug you will need to find another rescuer to express your negative emotions and satisfy your victimization. The rescuer gives you the permission to fail and not to change. Beware of false friends.

How many of us understand our own emotions, how many of us understand the importance of body language and how many know that body positions can affect the level of testosterone and cortisol in our brain and thus, may help to be successful.

Social psychologist Amy Cuddy focused her research on this subject. She came to the conclusion that standing in a posture of confidence would help people (even if not confident in themselves) to feel powerful and improve self-confidence.

We know that we have to focus on personal change rather than waiting for the environment and others to change us. We know many things in fact, but we do not change—what is the reason?

Imagine we are somebody blaming our parents as responsible of our failure, we think negatively, we have negative emotions (anger) and we feel bad in our body, we generate chemicals associated to these negative statements and we keep these thoughts and feelings during a decade or even more. These thoughts and feelings become our personality, as we always activate the same neuronal circuits. We became a negative person and we do not realize the fundamental reasons.

Let us take another example, when we read the news, journalists talk about terrorism, accidents, war, deaths, unemployment, etc.; these create fear, a negative emotion, we feel insecure, our body becomes rigid, our thoughts are negative, we generate more cortisol, all of these narrow our vision of the world and reduce our creativity, and we tend to focus on primary needs. If the war on terror lasts 20 years, we become addicted to security and fear. Our buying decisions are affected; our investment and holidays decisions are affected and obviously, our risk perception is affected. We become a negative person.

Even if the probability to die in a terror attack is low for many of us (I did not calculate the risk), the perception of the risk supersedes the real risk occurrence.

It is what you feel which creates your reality, not what is calculated logically.

When you buy a nice sport car, you buy the emotions associated to this car, not just the car. You create a movie where you are the actor, you imagine top models around you, drinking champagne and dressed like a fashion victim. Surely you will have power poses when driving your sport car. Now imagine that you drive a second-hand van, I think with a high probability that the picture of you will be dramatically different and your poses will be a bit humbler. We know that power poses, even if you are not a CEO or you are not the owner of a Ferrari, can help to reduce cortisol in your brain. It is free so let us use and abuse it.

We need to make an effort to be positive. Positive deep inside you, not simply a thin layer of positivity.

We all feel pain and with the same pain some people will suffer more than others; we call that resilience, the ability to recover quickly from an accident, drama, illness, job loss, or other change in life.

We talk about the personal changes, which as we can see are not straightforward because mainly we focus on one or few aspects of the system and the change is partial.

In order to really change, you need to take into consideration all aspects of YOU, your brain, your emotions, your body, because they all interact together.

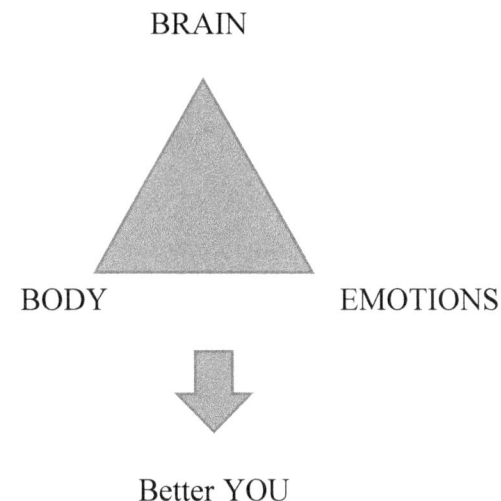

We forgot the holistic approach in many fields. A cohesive approach will drive you to change and will enable you to identify the deterministic zone in your life, the moment of change, the moment when you will become your ultimate observer and actor without dependency on others.

The change is about taking action, not just thinking and find justification. We are building the future in the present moment. Very often, we are in the past or in the future and we forget to appreciate the present moment. The only moment in time you are in control of is the present moment. Enjoy it!

The Four Dimensions of Corporate Changes

Dimension 1

In the first dimension of corporate changes, changes are related to peripheral changes such as: moving employees from one desk to another, changing a department from floor 3 to floor 6; or changing the titles of managers and staff.

In this dimension, there is a belief that a small change in the environment for the staff will create a sustained change for the company. The changes are imposed. There is also a code to be adopted to progress in the hierarchy, for example: behavior and language. Some expressions of the top Manager are reused by the courtesans; the global reality of the company is localized in the management meeting room. The managers spend the full day going from meeting to meeting with the goal of the day being able to attend all the meetings, resulting in more questions being minuted than solutions. Processes are generally very manual; staff and clients are not considered.

The communication about the company is not structured and no feedback loop to the top exists about the staff perception. In this context, the staff is dependent on the system, the self-esteem of the staff is decreasing. During a sustained period, there is a reverse reaction from the staff about the system as it has a perceived reliable control process, which helps unsecured staff to feel managed (by rules). For the management, the system is protected firmly as it is perceived as a rare opportunity for them to shine. The lack of confidence of the management in their inner quality renders the organization very rigid and focused on rules and policies. Bore out cases are frequent amongst qualified staff.

In this dimension, the attribute of power is very visible and the (morale) violence is present and obvious. The anthropologists say: it is with the violence that the society was created.

Dimension 2

In this dimension, some elements of the previous dimension persist. There is a timid opening to a specific category of the staff: the middle management and supervisors.

The participation of middle management at the meetings is a characteristic of this dimension, but only to reply to technical questions and make them accountable for the changes to be performed or of the issues the organization is facing.

The content of the black box (strategy and future) is shared with more people (the middle management) but the mandate to communicate the information remains with the senior management. Organization-wide communication comes from the Top and is ambiguous, including negative and positive statements in the same message.

On one side the middle management feels privileged to know a part of the secret, on the other side, they feel under high pressure due to the responsibilities transferred to them. Burn out cases are frequent amongst middle management.

From a perception of non-existence by the staff, the top management realizes that elements of opposition and reaction from staff can increase and affect the current equilibrium of the company. Fear is used increasingly to maintain the power.

This dimension is very often seen during economic downturn and crisis where staff reduction schemes and social plans are activated. It is like in the ancient worlds, when the society faced a critical moment (starvation, epidemics...), sacrifices where requested to appease the Gods. The lack of vision or strategy is not in question. Restructuration and social plans are modern sacrifices and it is a social act. Severe survival anxiety and lack of psychological safety amongst some middle management actors creates an identification with the hierarchy by taking their values and behavior. The negative role model facilitates cognitive redefinition amongst middle management.

Dimension 3

In this dimension, the management thinks the results of the sacrifice will become apparent. As the causes of the problems left the company (the sacrificed staff), the management organizes internal communication with all the staff, town hall meetings are scheduled, positive messages are conveyed. Management position themselves as the rescuer of the remaining staff not affected by the social plan; which leaves the staff as victims and the change will not happen.

It is implied that the changes are coming from the perception of the staff and that the bad moments have passed and they should be grateful to participate to the future of the organization.

Positivity cannot be created with negative memories. It is a false assumption to believe we are all equal to resilience.

Communication to staff increases and there is a request for feedback. New managers join the organization with more soft skills and people management skills. Although the majority of Management remains with the characteristics of the first two dimensions, creating a perceived inconsistency and a lack of managerial cohesive approach.

The changes are expected to be actioned by the staff as the management limits their change inputs to generic communication messages. The lack of positive role models prevents staff being motivated to change and be open to new information or learning. The survival anxiety remains too high compared to psychological safety to shift to a sustainable change model. Group of influence and individualism rather than team work is informally prone to slow down the change; however, we see the beginning of a paradigm shift.

Dimension 4

This is a radical change of paradigm compared to the first 3 dimensions. There is a totally different level of conscience which is taking place.

New types of managers are in place, which I call "wounded managers," conscious of their weaknesses and fully empathic to the staff. There is an optimal balance between psychological safety and survival anxiety. The wounded manager helps the staff to change their standards. Team work is the culture, the model of team work can be the special forces in the Army (Delta, Navy Seals). The best individual concept is the rule by encouraging the staff to be effective team players. The management agrees that the learning process is based on trial and error by scanning the broad environment for new concepts. During a period, the speed of change is too high to adopt a zero-default approach.

The dimension 4 organization creates a cohesive model were the added value of the human beings will focus on emotional performance with the support of artificial intelligence helping them to reduce psychological biases and a strong infrastructure and processes as the foundation.

The corporate cohesive model is similar to the personal cohesive approach of change.

Neurosciences and emotional performance will more and more be used by organizations.

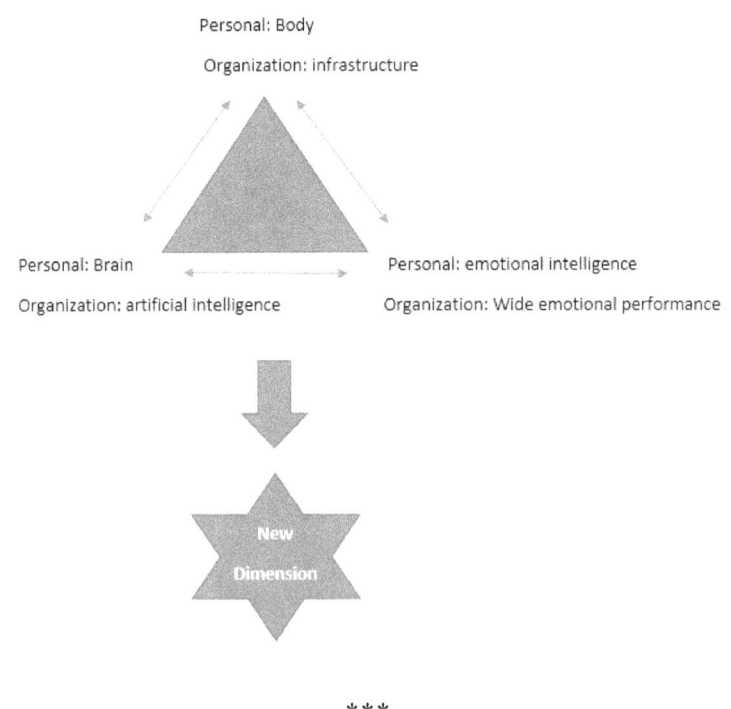

***

To Contact Yves:

Anacrouz.coaching@live.be

www.linkedin.com/in/yvesdeceuninck

Luxembourg: +352 621 73 74 58

Belgium: +32 475 23 20 62

AFTERWORD

Life is always a series of transitions… people, places, and things that shape who we are as individuals. Often, you never know that the next catalyst for change is around the corner.

Jim Britt and Jim Lutes have spent decades influencing individuals to blossom into the best version of themselves.

Allow all you have read in this book to create introspection and redirection if required. It's your journey to craft.

The Change is a series. A global movement. Watch for future releases and add them to your collection. If you know of anyone who would like to be considered as a co-author for a future book, have them email our offices at support@jimbritt.com.

The individual and combined works of Jim Britt and Jim Lutes have filled seminar rooms to maximum capacity and created a worldwide demand.

The blessings go both ways, as Jim and Jim are always willing students of life. Out of demand for life-changing programs and events, Jim and Jim conduct seminars and keynote presentations worldwide.

To Schedule Jim Britt or Jim Lutes as your featured speaker at your next convention or special event, or to organize and host a seminar in your area, email: support@jimbritt.com

Master your moment as they become hours that become days.

Your legacy awaits.

All the best,

Jim Britt and Jim Lutes

www.ingramcontent.com/pod-product-compliance
Lightning Source LLC
Chambersburg PA
CBHW052019070526
44584CB00016B/1823